EYEWITNESS VISUAL DICTIONARIES

THE VISUAL
DICTIONARY *of*
PHYSICS

Ammeter
shows that
current is
flowing

4.5V
battery

Current produces
magnetic field

Compass

Variable
resistor
adjusted to
allow current
to flow

Compass
needle aligns
with magnetic
field produced
by wire

ELECTROMAGNETISM AFFECTING A COMPASS NEEDLE

Glass tube

Clear plexiglass shield

Volume of trapped air

Column of oil

Connecting pipe

Bourdon gauge measures pressure

Rubber tubing

Foot pump

BOYLE'S LAW

Narrow tube

Upward meniscus forms

Glass

Drop of mercury

UPWARD MENISCUS

Ammeter measures current

Nichrome wire

Cell

Thick connecting wires have little resistance

OHM'S LAW

1-kg mass

Mass moves smoothly over surface

Steel roller

Flat surface

ROLLERS

LATENT HEAT

Thermometer reads 80.5°C

Temperature stays the same during melting

Beaker

Gauze

Liquid naphthalene

Solid naphthalene

Bunsen burner

1-kg mass

Rough sandpaper surface

Rough surface produces a lot of friction

FRICTION BETWEEN SURFACES

EYEWITNESS VISUAL DICTIONARIES

THE VISUAL
DICTIONARY *of*
PHYSICS

written by
Jack Challoner

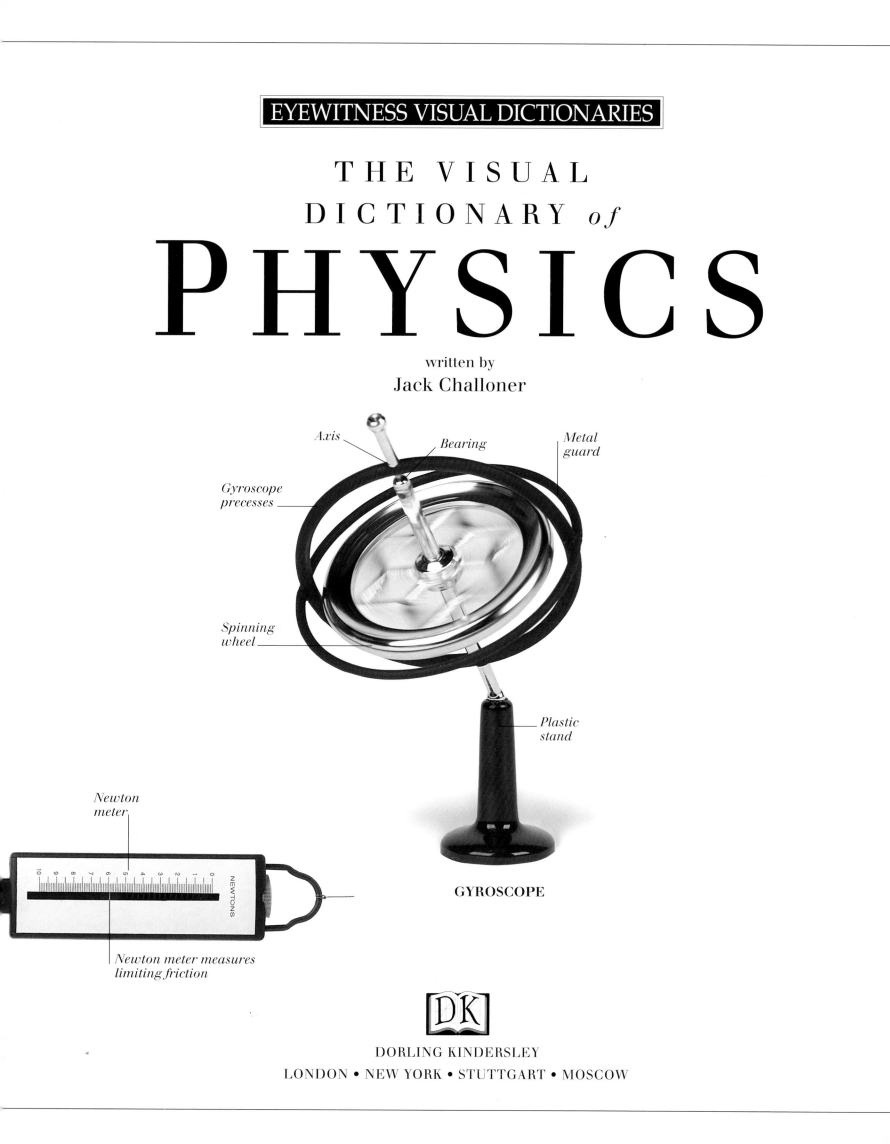

Axis

Bearing

Metal guard

Gyroscope precesses

Spinning wheel

Plastic stand

GYROSCOPE

Newton meter

NEWTONS

Newton meter measures limiting friction

DORLING KINDERSLEY
LONDON • NEW YORK • STUTTGART • MOSCOW

A DORLING KINDERSLEY BOOK

ART EDITOR SIMON MURRELL
PROJECT EDITOR PETER JONES
EDITORIAL ASSISTANT DES REID
US EDITOR JILL HAMILTON
US CONSULTANT META BROWN

DEPUTY ART DIRECTOR TINA VAUGHAN
MANAGING EDITOR SEAN MOORE
SENIOR ART EDITOR TRACY HAMBLETON-MILES

PHOTOGRAPHY ANDY CRAWFORD
ILLUSTRATIONS CHRIS LYON, JANOS MARFFY
PICTURE RESEARCH ANNA LORD
PRODUCTION MERYL SILBERT

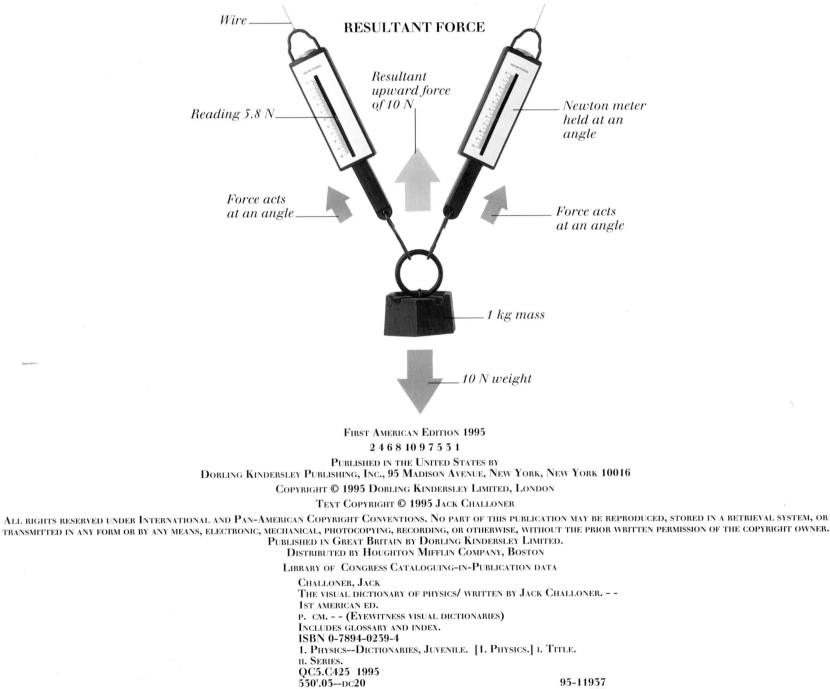

RESULTANT FORCE

Wire

Reading 5.8 N

Resultant upward force of 10 N

Newton meter held at an angle

Force acts at an angle

Force acts at an angle

1 kg mass

10 N weight

FIRST AMERICAN EDITION 1995

2 4 6 8 10 9 7 5 3 1

PUBLISHED IN THE UNITED STATES BY
DORLING KINDERSLEY PUBLISHING, INC., 95 MADISON AVENUE, NEW YORK, NEW YORK 10016

COPYRIGHT © 1995 DORLING KINDERSLEY LIMITED, LONDON

TEXT COPYRIGHT © 1995 JACK CHALLONER

PUBLISHED IN GREAT BRITAIN BY DORLING KINDERSLEY LIMITED.
DISTRIBUTED BY HOUGHTON MIFFLIN COMPANY, BOSTON

LIBRARY OF CONGRESS CATALOGUING-IN-PUBLICATION DATA

CHALLONER, JACK
THE VISUAL DICTIONARY OF PHYSICS/ WRITTEN BY JACK CHALLONER. - -
1ST AMERICAN ED.
P. CM. - - (EYEWITNESS VISUAL DICTIONARIES)
INCLUDES GLOSSARY AND INDEX.
ISBN 0-7894-0239-4
1. PHYSICS--DICTIONARIES, JUVENILE. [1. PHYSICS.] I. TITLE.
II. SERIES.
QC5.C425 1995
550'.03--DC20   95-11937
                                                  CIP
                                                  AC

REPRODUCED BY COLOURSCAN, SINGAPORE
PRINTED AND BOUND BY ARNOLDO MONDADORI, VERONA, ITALY

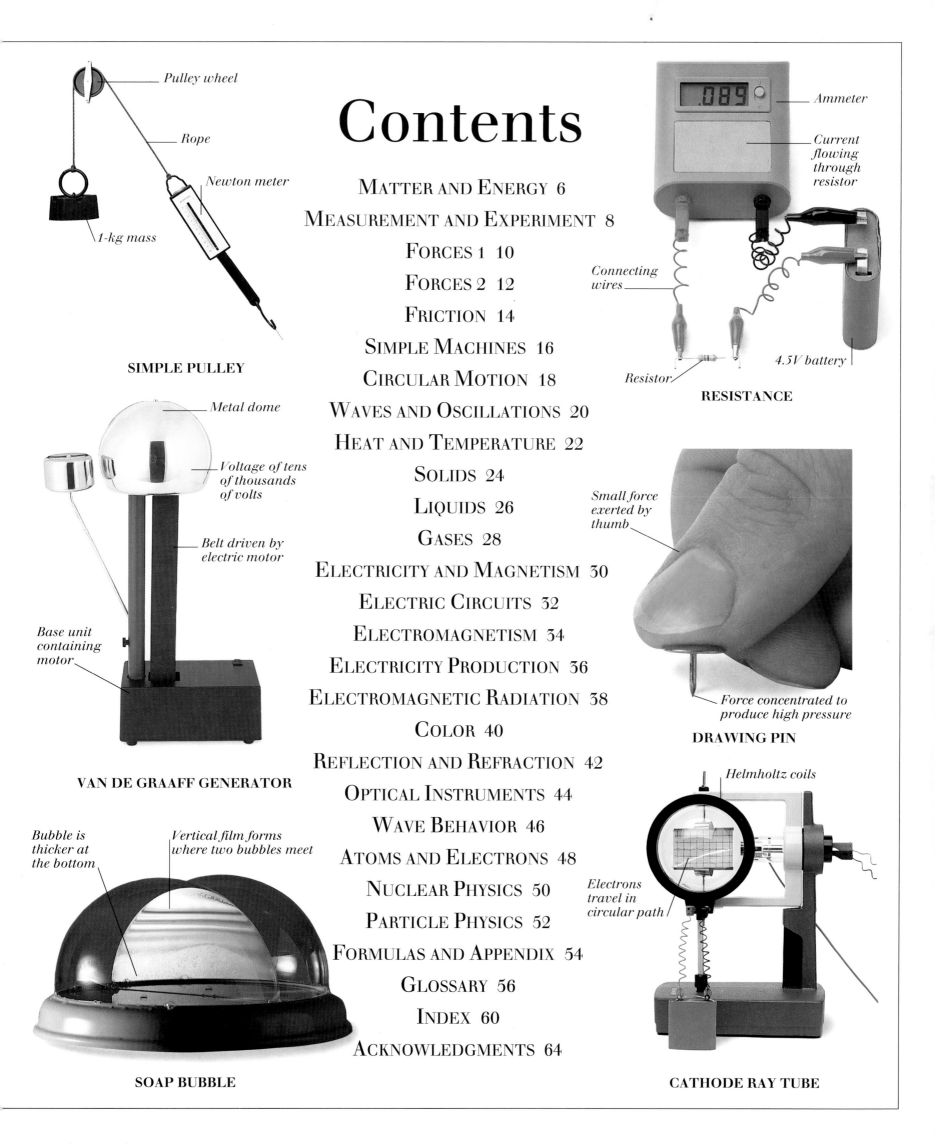

Pulley wheel

Rope

Newton meter

1-kg mass

SIMPLE PULLEY

Metal dome

Voltage of tens of thousands of volts

Belt driven by electric motor

Base unit containing motor

VAN DE GRAAFF GENERATOR

Bubble is thicker at the bottom

Vertical film forms where two bubbles meet

SOAP BUBBLE

Contents

Ammeter

Current flowing through resistor

Connecting wires

Resistor

4.5V battery

RESISTANCE

Small force exerted by thumb

Force concentrated to produce high pressure

DRAWING PIN

Helmholtz coils

Electrons travel in circular path

CATHODE RAY TUBE

Matter and energy

PHYSICS IS THE STUDY OF MATTER AND ENERGY. Matter is anything that occupies space. All matter consists of countless tiny particles, called **atoms** (see pp. 48–49) and **molecules**. These particles are in constant motion, a fact that explains a phenomenon known as **Brownian motion**. The existence of these particles also explains **evaporation** and the formation of **crystals** (see pp. 24–25). Energy is not matter, but it affects the behavior of matter. Everything that happens requires energy, and energy comes in many forms, such as heat, light, electrical, and potential energy. The standard unit for measuring energy is the joule (J). Each form of energy can change into other forms. For example, electrical energy used to make an electric motor turn becomes **kinetic energy** and heat energy (see pp. 22–23). The total amount of energy never changes; it can only be transferred from one form to another, not created or destroyed. This is known as the **Principle of the Conservation of Energy**, and can be illustrated using a **Sankey Diagram** (see opposite).

PARTICLES IN MOTION

BROWNIAN MOTION

When observed through a microscope, smoke particles are seen to move around randomly. This motion is caused by the air molecules around the smoke particles.

SMOKE CELL

Eyepiece

Glass compartment contains smoke

Light source

Objective lens

Smoke cell in place

Wires to battery

MICROSCOPE

MATTER AS PARTICLES

Air molecules in constant motion, nudge the smoke particle back and forth

Path of random movement

Smoke particle

UNDER THE MICROSCOPE

Air molecule

Air molecule bombards smoke particle

Smoke particle consists of atoms

Edge of smoke particle

BOMBARDMENT OF SMOKE PARTICLE

DISSOLVING

Glass beaker

Solid dissolves to form a solution

Water

Solid potassium manganate VII

Atom breaks away

Water molecule

Atoms at surface of solid

DISSOLVING
The particles of a solid are held together in a rigid structure. When a solid dissolves into a liquid, its particles break away from this structure and mix evenly in the liquid, forming a **solution**.

EVAPORATION

Heated liquid evaporates

Glass beaker

Dissolved solid does not evaporate

Solution is heated

Escaping water molecule

Air molecule

Water molecule evaporates

Surface of solution

Water molecule

Atom from solid in solution

EVAPORATION
When they are heated, most liquids **evaporate**. This means that the atoms or molecules of which they are made break free from the body of the liquid to become gas particles.

CRYSTALLIZATION

Glass beaker

Water has evaporated

Purple crystals of potassium manganate VII remain behind

Solid particle adds on to structure

Regular crystal structure

Surface of solid

CRYSTALLIZATION
When all of the liquid in a solution has evaporated, the solid is left behind. The particles of the solid normally arrange in a regular structure, called a crystal.

THE CONSERVATION OF ENERGY

— Sun

Energy radiates into space

Radiation is made in the Sun's core during nuclear reactions and is the source of most of the Earth's energy

PHOTOVOLTAIC CELL
A transfer of energy, from electromagnetic radiation to electrical energy, takes place in a photovoltaic cell, or solar cell. When no sunlight falls on it, it can supply no electricity.

Solar cell

Wire from cell to motor

Silicon crystal

At each energy transfer some energy is "lost" as heat

ELECTRIC MOTOR
Inside an electric motor, electrical energy becomes the energy of movement, also known as kinetic or mechanical energy.

Motor

The faster the motor turns, the more energy it has

Motor's spindle turns gears

Worm gear

Crown wheel

String winds around shaft

ENERGY TRANSFER

SANKEY DIAGRAM
This Sankey diagram shows the energy transfers in an electric motor.

Width of the arrow here shows how much energy is available

0.31 J of electrical energy supplied each second

0.1 J of kinetic energy

Arrowhead shows where energy is transferred

0.21 J wasted as heat in the motor

POTENTIAL ENERGY
As the motor turns, it winds a string around a shaft via a set of gears. The string lifts a 0.1-kilogram mass against **gravity**. The kinetic energy transfers to potential, or stored energy. If the string is broken, the energy will be released, and the mass will fall, gaining kinetic energy.

0.1-kg mass lifted to 1 m

Mass has potential energy of 1 J

String lifts 0.1-kg mass

Mass has potential energy of 0.9 J

1-kg mass lifted to 0.9 m

Mass has potential energy of 0.8 J

0.1-kg mass lifted to 0.8 m

0.1-kg mass

ENERGY TRANSFERS IN A CAR

A car's energy comes from burning gasoline in the engine. This includes the electrical energy in its battery, the **potential energy** stored as it climbs a hill, and any heat generated in the brakes or the engine. The arrows show energy transfer.

Gasoline (chemical energy)

Climbing a hill (potential energy)

Car stereo (electrical to sound energy)

Car battery (electrical energy)

Heat energy generated in engine

Headlights (electrical to light energy)

Kinetic energy greater at higher speed

Braking (heat energy)

7

Measurement and experiment

THE SCIENCE OF PHYSICS IS BASED on the formulation and testing of theories. Experiments are designed to test theories and involve making measurements: of **mass**, length, time, or other quantities. In order to compare the results of various experiments, standard units are necessary. The kilogram (kg), the meter (m), and the second (s) are the fundamental units of a system called **SI units** (Système International). Physicists use a variety of instruments for making measurements. Some, like the Vernier callipers, traveling microscopes, and thermometers are common to many laboratories, while others will be made for a particular experiment. The results of measurements are interpreted in many ways, but most often as graphs. Graphs provide a way of illustrating the relationship between two measurements involved in an experiment. For example, in an experiment to investigate falling objects, a graph can show the relationship between the duration and the height of the fall.

MASS AND WEIGHT
Mass is the amount of matter in an object, and is measured in kilograms. **Gravitational force** gives the mass its **weight**. Weight is a force, and is measured in newtons (see pp.10–11), using a newton meter like the one shown on the right. It is common to speak of weight being measured in kilograms, but in physics this is not correct.

Spring stretches

Pointer moves down scale

Pointer reads 10 N

Spring in meter produces force to balance weight

1-kg mass

Fulcrum

SCALES
The metal object and the powder shown here have the same mass and therefore the same weight.

Metal object

0.2-kg mass

0.2-kg mass

Powder to be weighed

Scale pan

NEWTON METER AND KILOGRAM MASS

MEASURING DISTANCE

Jaws measure either internal or external diameter of object

Jaws

VERNIER CALLIPERS
Physicists often use Vernier callipers for the accurate measurement of an object's width. This is read off a **Vernier scale,** which here allows reading to an accuracy of 0.1 mm.

Measured object

Vernier scale

Ordinary scale

Adjustable eyepiece

Eyepiece contains fine crossed wires

TRAVELING MICROSCOPE
A Vernier scale makes the traveling microscope an accurate instrument for measuring small distances across objects. Two readings are taken and the difference between the positions of the microscope on its sliding scale provides the measurement.

Focusing knob

Diecast body

Vernier scale

Ordinary scale

Microscope body

Microscope slides on rails

Turning knob moves microscope along rails

Objective lens

THERMOMETERS

There are two types of thermometer commonly used in modern physics. The mercury thermometer has a glass bulb containing mercury that expands as the temperature rises, while the digital thermometer contains an electronic probe and has a digital readout.

DIGITAL THERMOMETER

Mercury column

Electronic probe

Digital (LCD) readout

Plastic case contains electronics

Glass tube

MERCURY THERMOMETER

Scale

Mercury bulb

Human body temperature (37°C)

Glass tube

MAGNIFIED VIEW OF MERCURY THERMOMETER

Glass bulb

FREEFALL EXPERIMENT

Electromagnet

Ring stand

Steel ball is held up by electromagnet

Clamp

Steel ball

Wire from second switch

INTERPRETING DATA

TABLE OF RESULTS FOR A FREEFALL EXPERIMENT

A steel ball is dropped from a variety of heights and the duration of each fall is timed. The results of these measurements are entered into a table.

HEIGHT (m)	0	0.05	0.10	0.15	0.20	0.25	0.30	0.35	0.40	0.45	0.50
TIME (s)	0	0.10	0.14	0.17	0.21	0.22	0.24	0.26	0.27	0.30	0.31

RESULTS OF A FREEFALL EXPERIMENT IN GRAPH FORM

A **graph** allows us to identify visually the relationship between the time and the height of the fall. There is an element of uncertainty or error in every result obtained, so each is plotted on the graph as a short range of values forming an **error bar** instead of a point. The curve is drawn so that it passes through all the bars.

Y-axis

"Best fit" curve

Result is plotted as a short range of values

Ball approaches terminal velocity

Bars show margin of error

Some points fall below curve

Some points fall above curve

Duration of fall (s)

X-axis **Height of fall (m)**

Ball accelerates due to the pull of gravity

APPARATUS FOR TIMING THE FALL OF AN OBJECT

A switch turns off the electromagnet, releasing the ball while simultaneously starting the timer. As the ball hits the ring stand base, a second switch is activated, and the timer stops. Times of falls from various heights are measured, and plotted on a graph (see left).

As ball hits base, second switch is activated

Second switch (two contacts normally held apart)

Ring stand base

Wire from first switch

Electronic timer

Wire to battery

Electronic timer stand

Digital display

Wire from second switch

Switch

Alligator clip

Forces 1

A FORCE IS A PUSH OR PULL, and can be large or small. The usual unit of force is the newton (N), and forces can be measured using a **newton meter** (see pp. 8–9). Force can be applied to objects at a distance or by making contact. **Gravity** (see pp. 12–13) and **electromagnetism** (see pp. 34–35) are examples of forces that can act at a distance. When more than one force acts on an object, the combined force is called the **resultant**. The resultant of several forces depends on their size and direction. The object is in **equilibrium** if the forces on an object are balanced with no overall resultant. An object on a solid flat surface will be in equilibrium, because the surface produces a **reaction** force to balance the object's **weight**. If the surface slopes, the object's weight is no longer completely cancelled by the reaction force and part of the weight, called a **component**, remains, pulling the object toward the bottom of the slope. Forces can cause rotation as well as straight line motion. If an object is free to rotate about a certain point, then a force can have a turning effect, known as a **moment**.

RESULTANT FORCE

A 1-kg **mass** has a weight of 10 N. Here, this weight is supported by two lengths of wire. Each wire carries a force that pulls against the other at an angle. The combination or resultant of these forces is 10 N vertically upward and exactly balances the weight. The force carried by each wire is measured by newton meters.

Wire

Newton meters held at an angle

Resultant upward force of 10 N exactly balances 10 N weight

Reading 5.8 N

Reading 5.8 N

Force acts at an angle

Force acts at an angle

THE METER READINGS
Between them, the two wires support a weight of 10 N, so why is the reading on each newton meter more than 5 N? In addition to pulling upward, the wires are pulling sideways against each other, so the overall force showing on each meter is 5.8 N.

1-kg mass

10-N weight

REACTION FORCES

FORCES ON A LEVEL SURFACE
A table provides a force called a reaction, which exactly balances the weight of an object placed upon it. The resultant force is zero, so the object does not fall through the table.

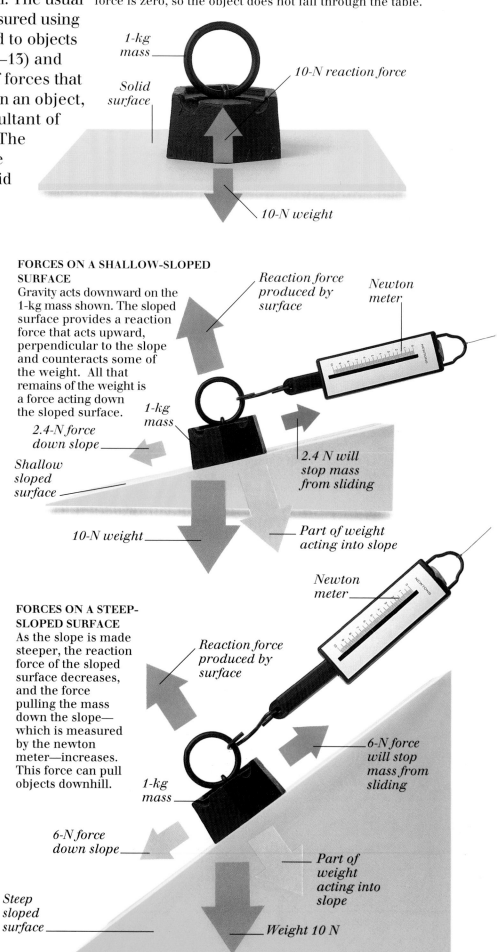

1-kg mass

Solid surface

10-N reaction force

10-N weight

FORCES ON A SHALLOW-SLOPED SURFACE
Gravity acts downward on the 1-kg mass shown. The sloped surface provides a reaction force that acts upward, perpendicular to the slope and counteracts some of the weight. All that remains of the weight is a force acting down the sloped surface.

Reaction force produced by surface

Newton meter

1-kg mass

2.4-N force down slope

Shallow sloped surface

2.4 N will stop mass from sliding

10-N weight

Part of weight acting into slope

FORCES ON A STEEP-SLOPED SURFACE
As the slope is made steeper, the reaction force of the sloped surface decreases, and the force pulling the mass down the slope— which is measured by the newton meter—increases. This force can pull objects downhill.

Newton meter

Reaction force produced by surface

1-kg mass

6-N force will stop mass from sliding

6-N force down slope

Part of weight acting into slope

Steep sloped surface

Weight 10 N

TURNING FORCES

TURNING FORCES AROUND A PIVOT

A force acting on an object that is free to rotate will have a turning effect, or turning force, also known as a moment. The moment of a force is equal to the size of the force multiplied by the distance of the force from the turning point around which it acts (see p. 54). It is measured in newton meters (Nm). The mass below exerts a weight of 10 N downward on a pivoted beam. The newton meter—twice as far from the pivot—measures 5 N, the upward force needed to stop the beam turning. The clockwise moment created by the weight and counterclockwise moment created by the upward pull on the newton meter are equal, and the object is therefore in equilibrium.

Ring stand

Weight 10 N, 0.25 m from the pivot

1-kg mass

Newton meter

Reading 5 N

Upward force 5 N, 0.5 m from the pivot

Pivot point

Clockwise moment, 2.5 Nm (10 N x 0.25 m)

Counterclockwise moment, 2.5 Nm (5 N x 0.5 m)

OBJECT SUSPENDED AT CENTER OF GRAVITY

Counterclockwise moment   *Suspended at center of gravity*   *Clockwise moment*

The weight of the beam above is spread along its length. The moments are balanced if the object is suspended at its center of gravity.

OBJECT SUSPENDED AWAY FROM CENTER OF GRAVITY

Point of suspension   *Center of gravity*   *Resultant turning effect*

Center of gravity

Beam

Weight of beam

When this beam is suspended at a point away from its **center of gravity**, there is a resultant turning effect.

The beam turns until the center of gravity is under the point of suspension

PRESSURE

Why can a drawing pin be pushed into a wall, and yet a building will not sink into the ground? Forces can act over large or small areas. A force acting over a large area will exert less **pressure** than the same force acting over a small area. The pressure exerted on an area can be worked out simply by dividing the applied force by the area over which it acts (see p. 54). Pressure is normally measured in units of newtons per square meter (Nm^{-2}). A drawing pin concentrates force to produce high pressure, whereas the foundations of a building spread the load to reduce pressure. Gases also exert pressure (see pp. 28–29).

Mass of block 2 kg   *Weight of block 20 N*

Block

Mass of block 1 kg   *Weight of block 10 N*

Block

Block

Small force exerted by thumb

Tiny area at pin point concentrates force to produce high pressure

DRAWING PIN

Mass of block 2 kg

Weight of block 20 N

Pressure exerted 80 Nm^{-2} (20 N ÷ 0.25m²)

Pressure exerted 40 Nm^{-2} (10 N ÷ 0.25 m²)

Pressure exerted 40 Nm^{-2} (20 N ÷ 0.5 m²)

Area of base 0.25 m²

Area of base 0.25 m²

Area of base 0.5 m²

Grid with squares of area 0.01 m²

Forces 2

WHEN THE FORCES ON AN OBJECT do not cancel each other out, they will change the motion of the object. The object's speed, direction of motion, or both will change. The rules governing the way forces change the motion of objects were first worked out by Sir Isaac Newton. They have become known as Newton's Laws. The greater the mass of an object, the greater the force needed to change its motion. This resistance to change in motion is called **inertia**. The **speed** of an object is usually measured in meters per second (ms^{-1}). **Velocity** is the speed of an object in a particular direction. **Acceleration**, which only occurs when a force is applied, is the rate of change in speed. It is measured in meters per second per second, or meters per second squared (ms^{-2}). One particular force keeps the Moon in orbit around the Earth and the Earth in orbit around the Sun. This is the force of **gravity** or **gravitation**; its effects can be felt over great distances.

NEWTON'S SECOND LAW IN ACTION
Trucks have a greater mass than cars. According to Newton's second law (see right) a large mass requires a larger force to produce a given acceleration. This is why a truck needs to have a larger engine than a car.

Car — Small mass — Small engine

Truck — Large mass

Large engine

NEWTON'S LAWS

NEWTON'S FIRST LAW
When no force acts on an object, it will remain in a state of rest or continue its uniform motion in a straight line.

No force acts on cart — Cart is stationary

No force, no acceleration: state of rest

No force acts on cart — Cart is moving at constant speed

No force, no acceleration: uniform motion

NEWTON'S SECOND LAW
When a force acts on an object, the motion of the object will change. This change in motion is called acceleration and is equal to the size of the force divided by the mass of the object on which it acts (see p. 54).

Spring exerts force on cart — Cart accelerates only when force acts on it — Cart with small mass accelerates to a high speed

Force acts on small mass: large acceleration

Mass on cart — Same force acts on heavier cart — Cart with large mass accelerates to a low speed

Same force acts on large mass: small acceleration

NEWTON'S THIRD LAW
If one object exerts a force on another, an equal and opposite force, called the reaction force, is applied by the second to the first.

First cart moves to left — Spring exerts force to the left on first cart — An equal and opposite reaction force acts on the right-hand cart — Second cart moves to right

Action and reaction

FORCE AND MOTION

In the images below, each row of balls is a record of the motion of one ball, photographed once each second beside a ruler. This shows how far the ball moved during that second and each subsequent second, giving a visual representation of speed and acceleration.

SPEED

Speed is the distance an object travels in a set amount of time. It is calculated by dividing distance covered by time taken (see p. 54). In physics, speed is measured in meters per second (ms^{-1}).

Ruler

Ball

After 6 seconds, ball has moved 6 meters

Ball traveling at 1 ms^{-1}

Ball

After 3 seconds, ball has moved 6 meters

Ball traveling at 2 ms^{-1}

ACCELERATION

Acceleration is the rate that the speed of an object changes. It is calculated by dividing the change in speed by the time it took for that change (see p. 54). It is measured in meters per second per second (ms^{-2}).

Ruler

Ball accelerating at 1 ms^{-2}

After 2 seconds, the ball is moving at 2 ms^{-1}

After 4 seconds, the ball is moving at 4 ms^{-1}

MOMENTUM

The momentum of an object is equal to its mass multiplied by its velocity (see p. 54). Momentum is measured in kilogram meters per second ($kgms^{-1}$). The two balls below have the same momentum.

Ruler

Ball, mass 1 kg

Ball traveling at 1 ms^{-1}

Momentum 1 $kgms^{-1}$

Ball, mass 0.5 kg

Ball traveling at 2 ms^{-1}

Momentum 1 $kgms^{-1}$

NEWTON'S SECOND LAW APPLIED TO ACCELERATION

BALL ACCELERATES AT 1 ms^{-2}

Force of 1 N

Ball, mass 1 kg

Ball reaches 5 ms^{-1} after 5 seconds

BALL ACCELERATES AT 2 ms^{-2}

Force of 2 N

Ball, mass 1 kg

Twice the force produces twice the acceleration

BALL ACCELERATES AT 1 ms^{-2}

Force of 2 N

Ball, mass 2 kg

Doubling both force and mass leaves acceleration unchanged

GRAVITATIONAL FORCE

Gravitation, or gravity, is a force that acts on all matter. The force between any two objects depends upon their masses and the distance between them (see p. 54).

Earth

Distance

Moon

Moon exerts force on Earth

Earth exerts force on Moon

If the Moon had twice the mass that it does, the force between the Earth and Moon would be twice as large.

Earth

Moon

Twice the force

Twice the mass

If the Moon were half the distance from the Earth, the gravitational force would be four times as large. This is because the force depends upon the square of the distance.

Earth

Four times the force

Half the distance

Moon

Friction

FRICTION IS A FORCE THAT SLOWS DOWN or prevents motion. A familiar form of friction is air resistance, which limits the speed at which objects can move through the air. Between touching surfaces, the amount of friction depends on the nature of the surfaces and the force or forces pushing them together. It is the joining or bonding of the **atoms** at each of the surfaces that causes the friction. When you try to pull an object along a table, the object will not move until the **limiting friction** supplied by these bonds has been overcome. Friction can be reduced in two main ways: by lubrication or by the use of rollers. Lubrication involves the presence of a **fluid** between two surfaces; fluid keeps the surfaces apart, allowing them to move smoothly past one another. Rollers actually use friction to grip the surfaces and produce rotation. Instead of sliding against one another, the surfaces produce turning forces, which cause each roller to roll. This leaves very little friction to oppose motion.

AIR RESISTANCE

Air resistance is a type of friction that occurs when an object moves through the air. The faster an object moves, the greater the air resistance. Falling objects accelerate to a speed called **terminal velocity**, at which the air resistance exactly balances the object's weight. At this speed, there is no **resultant force** and so no further acceleration can occur.

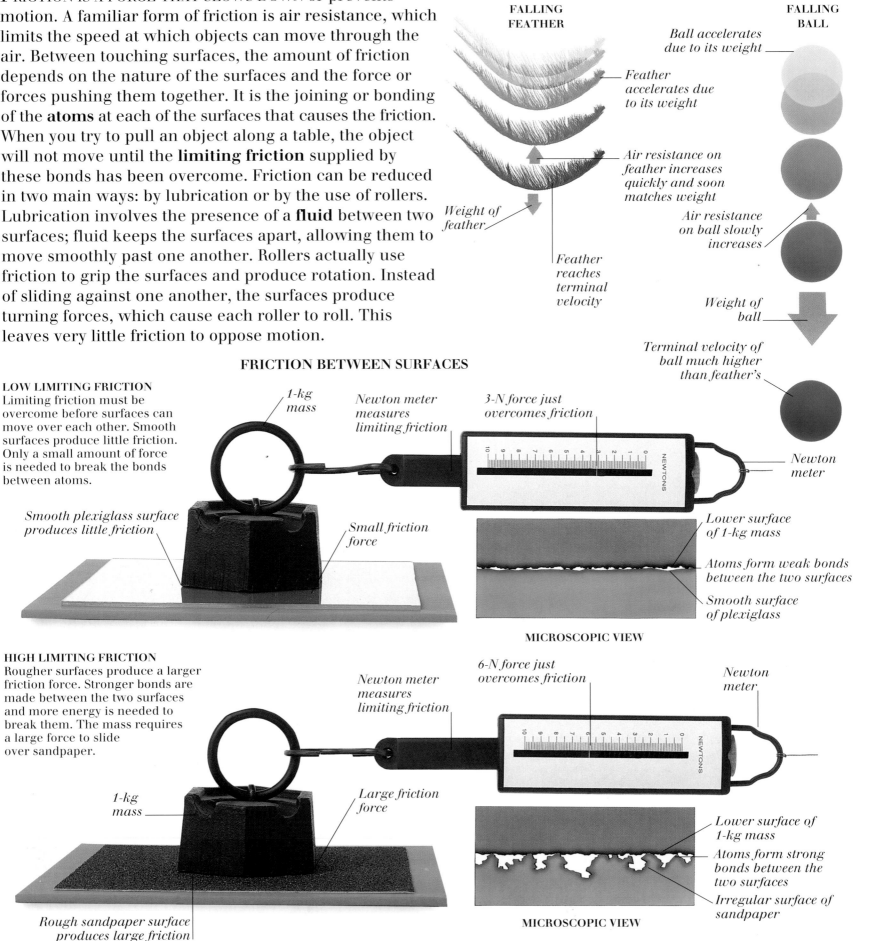

FALLING FEATHER

Feather accelerates due to its weight

Air resistance on feather increases quickly and soon matches weight

Weight of feather

Feather reaches terminal velocity

FALLING BALL

Ball accelerates due to its weight

Air resistance on ball slowly increases

Weight of ball

Terminal velocity of ball much higher than feather's

FRICTION BETWEEN SURFACES

LOW LIMITING FRICTION
Limiting friction must be overcome before surfaces can move over each other. Smooth surfaces produce little friction. Only a small amount of force is needed to break the bonds between atoms.

1-kg mass

Newton meter measures limiting friction

3-N force just overcomes friction

Newton meter

Smooth plexiglass surface produces little friction

Small friction force

Lower surface of 1-kg mass

Atoms form weak bonds between the two surfaces

Smooth surface of plexiglass

MICROSCOPIC VIEW

HIGH LIMITING FRICTION
Rougher surfaces produce a larger friction force. Stronger bonds are made between the two surfaces and more energy is needed to break them. The mass requires a large force to slide over sandpaper.

1-kg mass

Newton meter measures limiting friction

6-N force just overcomes friction

Newton meter

Large friction force

Lower surface of 1-kg mass

Atoms form strong bonds between the two surfaces

Irregular surface of sandpaper

Rough sandpaper surface produces large friction

MICROSCOPIC VIEW

MOTORCYCLE BRAKE

Friction is put to good use in the disk brakes of a motorcycle. The friction force between disk and brake pad slows down the rotation of the wheel, reducing the vehicle's speed. In doing so, it converts the **kinetic energy** of the vehicle into heat (see p. 7).

Piston

Caliper unit

Brake pad (inside caliper unit)

Metal brake disk

BALL BEARINGS

Bearings are a type of roller used to reduce friction between moving machine parts such as a wheel and its axle. As a wheel turns on its axle, the balls roll around inside the bearing, drastically reducing the friction between wheel and axle.

Hub

Ball race

Ball bearing

LUBRICATION
The presence of oil or another fluid between two surfaces keeps the surfaces apart. Because fluids (liquids or gases) flow, they allow movement between surfaces. Here, a lubricated kilogram mass slides down a slope, while an unlubricated one is prevented from moving by friction.

Unlubricated mass remains stationary

Patch of oil reduces friction

High friction prevents mass from moving

Inclined plane

1-kg mass

Lubricated mass moves down slope

ROLLERS

THE ACTION OF A ROLLER ON A SLOPE
Friction causes the roller to grip the slope so that it turns. If there were no friction, the roller would simply slide down the slope.

Roller

Force down the slope

Shallow slope

Frictional force

1-kg mass

Steel roller

Flat surface

USING ROLLERS TO AVOID FRICTION
Rollers placed between two surfaces keep the surfaces apart. The rollers allow the underside of the kilogram mass to move freely over the ground. An object placed on rollers will move smoothly if pushed or pulled.

Friction forces between surfaces create a turning force that turns the rollers

Mass moves smoothly over surface

Underside of 1-kg mass

Simple machines

IN PHYSICS, A MACHINE IS ANY DEVICE that can be used to transmit a **force** (see pp. 10–11) and, in doing so, change its size or direction. When using a simple pulley, a type of machine, a person can lift a load by pulling downward on the rope. By using several pulleys connected together as a block and tackle, the size of the force can be changed too, so that a heavy load can be lifted using a small force. Other simple machines include the inclined plane, the lever, the screw, and the wheel and axle. All of these machines illustrate the concept of **work**. Work is the amount of energy expended when a force is moved through a distance. The force applied to a machine is called the effort, while the force it overcomes is called the load. The effort is often smaller than the load, for a small effort can overcome a heavy load if the effort is moved through a larger distance. The machine is then said to give a mechanical advantage. Although the effort will be smaller when using a machine, the amount of work done, or energy used, will be equal to or greater than that without the machine.

AN INCLINED PLANE
The force needed to drag an object up a slope is less than that needed to lift it vertically. However, the distance moved by the object is greater when pulled up the slope than if it were lifted vertically.

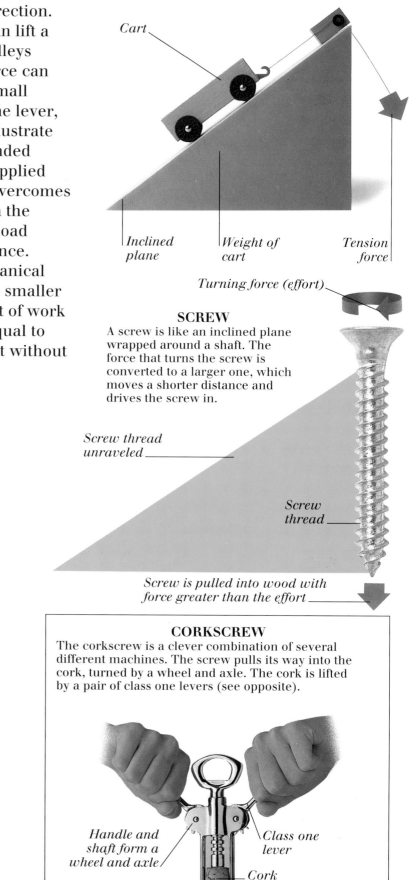

Cart

Inclined plane *Weight of cart* *Tension force*

Turning force (effort)

SCREW
A screw is like an inclined plane wrapped around a shaft. The force that turns the screw is converted to a larger one, which moves a shorter distance and drives the screw in.

Screw thread unraveled

Screw thread

Screw is pulled into wood with force greater than the effort

Ax handle

WEDGE
The ax is a wedge. The applied force moves a long way into the wood, producing a larger force, which pushes the wood apart a short distance.

Metal ax blade

Small force applied

Block of wood

Large force produced

Wood splits apart

CORKSCREW
The corkscrew is a clever combination of several different machines. The screw pulls its way into the cork, turned by a wheel and axle. The cork is lifted by a pair of class one levers (see opposite).

Handle and shaft form a wheel and axle

Class one lever

Cork

Neck of bottle

Screw

PULLEYS

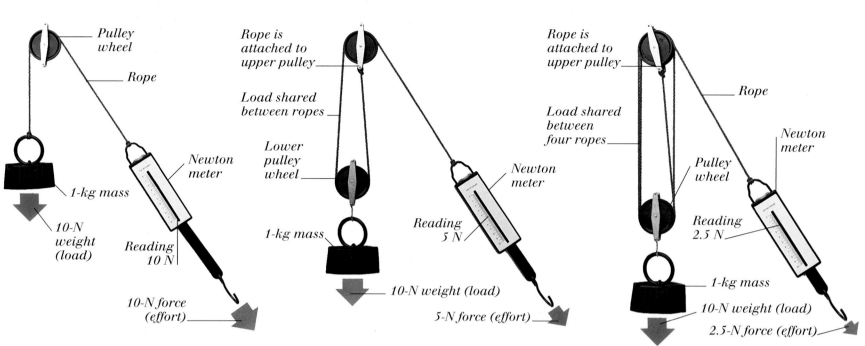

SIMPLE PULLEY
A simple pulley changes the direction of a force but not its size. Here a one-kg mass, weighing ten newtons, is lifted by a ten-newton force. The mass and the other end of the rope move through the same distance.

DOUBLE PULLEY
A double pulley will lift a one-kg mass with only a five-newton effort, because the force in the rope doubles up as the rope does. However, pulling the rope by one meter only raises the mass by half a meter.

QUADRUPLE PULLEY
Lifting a one-kg mass with a quadruple pulley, in which the rope goes over four pulley wheels, feels almost effortless. However, pulling the rope by one meter lifts the mass by only one quarter of a meter.

THREE CLASSES OF LEVER

CLASS ONE LEVER
In a class one lever, the **fulcrum** (pivot point) is between the effort and the load. The load is larger than the effort, but it moves through a smaller distance.

CLASS TWO LEVER
In a class two lever, the load is between the fulcrum and effort. Here again, the load is greater than the effort and it moves through a smaller distance.

CLASS THREE LEVER
In a class three lever, the effort is between the fulcrum and the load. In this case, the load is less than the effort but it moves through a greater distance.

WHEEL AND AXLE
As the pedal and chainwheel of a bicycle turn through one revolution, the pedal moves farther than the links of the chain. For this reason, the force applied to the chain is greater than the force applied to the pedal. The steering wheel of a car is another example of a wheel and axle.

Circular motion

WHEN AN OBJECT MOVES IN A CIRCLE, its direction is continuously changing. Any change in direction requires a **force** (see pp. 12–13). The force required to maintain circular motion is called **centripetal force**. The size of this force depends on the size of the circle and the mass and speed of the object (see p. 54). The centripetal force that keeps an object whirling around on the end of a string is caused by **tension** (see pp. 24–25) in the string. When the centripetal force ceases—for example, if the string breaks— the object flies off in a straight line, since no force is acting upon it. **Gravity** (see pp. 10–11) is the centripetal force that keeps planets such as the Earth in orbit around the Sun. Without this centripetal force, the Earth would move in a straight line through space. On a smaller scale, without friction to provide centripetal force, a motorcyclist could not steer around a corner. Spinning, a form of circular motion, gives **gyroscopes** stability.

CENTRIPETAL FORCE

In the experiment below, centripetal force is provided by tension in a length of string, which keeps a 1-kg mass moving in a circle. The mass can move freely as it floats like a hovercraft on the jets of air supplied from beneath it. When the circle is twice as large, half the force is needed. However, moving twice as fast requires four times the force (see p. 54).

CONTROL EXPERIMENT

Speed of object 1 ms⁻¹

Radius of circle 0.2 m

1-kg mass

Frictionless table

Air hole

5-N tension provides the centripetal force

TWICE THE SPEED, FOUR TIMES THE FORCE

Speed of object 2 ms⁻¹

Radius of circle 0.2 m

1-kg mass

20-N centripetal force

Higher speed requires greater centripetal force

TWICE THE RADIUS, HALF THE FORCE

Speed of object 1 ms⁻¹

1-kg mass

Radius of circle 0.4 m

2.5-N centripetal force

Larger radius requires smaller centripetal force

MOTION IN A CIRCLE

ASPECTS OF CIRCULAR MOTION

The force that continuously changes the direction of an object moving in a circle is called centripetal force. It is directed toward the center of the circle. The smaller the radius of the circle, the larger the force needed.

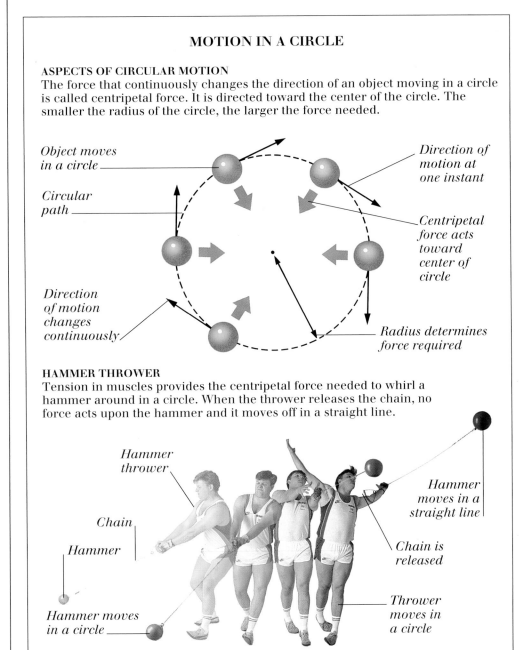

Object moves in a circle

Circular path

Direction of motion changes continuously

Direction of motion at one instant

Centripetal force acts toward center of circle

Radius determines force required

HAMMER THROWER

Tension in muscles provides the centripetal force needed to whirl a hammer around in a circle. When the thrower releases the chain, no force acts upon the hammer and it moves off in a straight line.

Hammer thrower

Chain

Hammer

Hammer moves in a circle

Hammer moves in a straight line

Chain is released

Thrower moves in a circle

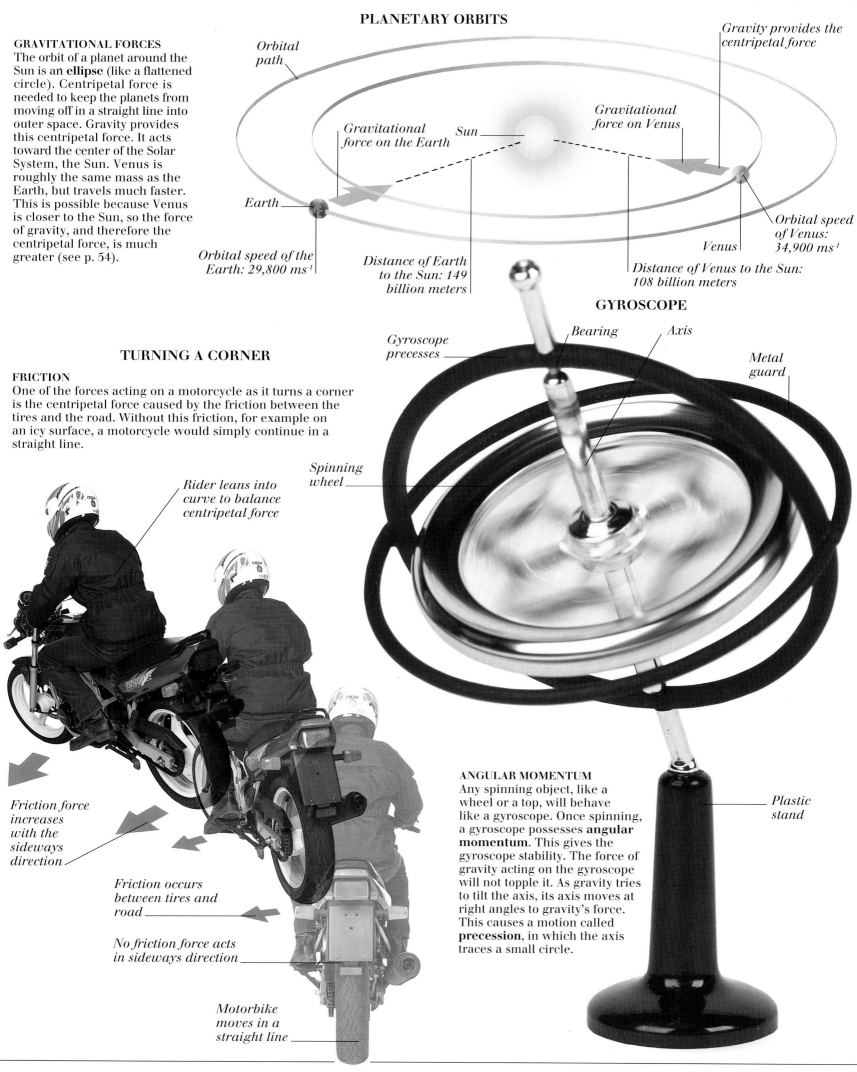

PLANETARY ORBITS

GRAVITATIONAL FORCES
The orbit of a planet around the Sun is an **ellipse** (like a flattened circle). Centripetal force is needed to keep the planets from moving off in a straight line into outer space. Gravity provides this centripetal force. It acts toward the center of the Solar System, the Sun. Venus is roughly the same mass as the Earth, but travels much faster. This is possible because Venus is closer to the Sun, so the force of gravity, and therefore the centripetal force, is much greater (see p. 54).

Orbital path

Gravity provides the centripetal force

Gravitational force on the Earth

Sun

Gravitational force on Venus

Earth

Orbital speed of the Earth: 29,800 ms⁻¹

Distance of Earth to the Sun: 149 billion meters

Venus

Distance of Venus to the Sun: 108 billion meters

Orbital speed of Venus: 34,900 ms⁻¹

TURNING A CORNER

FRICTION
One of the forces acting on a motorcycle as it turns a corner is the centripetal force caused by the friction between the tires and the road. Without this friction, for example on an icy surface, a motorcycle would simply continue in a straight line.

Rider leans into curve to balance centripetal force

Friction force increases with the sideways direction

Friction occurs between tires and road

No friction force acts in sideways direction

Motorbike moves in a straight line

GYROSCOPE

Gyroscope precesses

Bearing

Axis

Metal guard

Spinning wheel

ANGULAR MOMENTUM
Any spinning object, like a wheel or a top, will behave like a gyroscope. Once spinning, a gyroscope possesses **angular momentum**. This gives the gyroscope stability. The force of gravity acting on the gyroscope will not topple it. As gravity tries to tilt the axis, its axis moves at right angles to gravity's force. This causes a motion called **precession**, in which the axis traces a small circle.

Plastic stand

Waves and oscillations

AN **OSCILLATION** IS ANY MOTION BACK AND FORTH, such as that of a pendulum. When that motion travels through matter or space, it becomes a wave. An oscillation, or vibration, occurs when a force acts that pulls a displaced object back to its **equilibrium** position, and the size of this force increases with the size of the **displacement**. A **mass** on a spring, for example, is acted upon by two forces: **gravity** and the **tension** (see pp. 28–29) in the spring. At the point of equilibrium, the **resultant** (see pp. 10–11) of these forces is zero: they cancel each other out. At all other points, the resultant force acts in a direction that restores the object to its equilibrium. This results in the object moving back and forth, or oscillating, about that position. Vibration is very common, and results in the phenomenon of sound. In air, the vibrations that cause sound are transmitted as a wave between air molecules; many other substances transmit sound in a similar way.

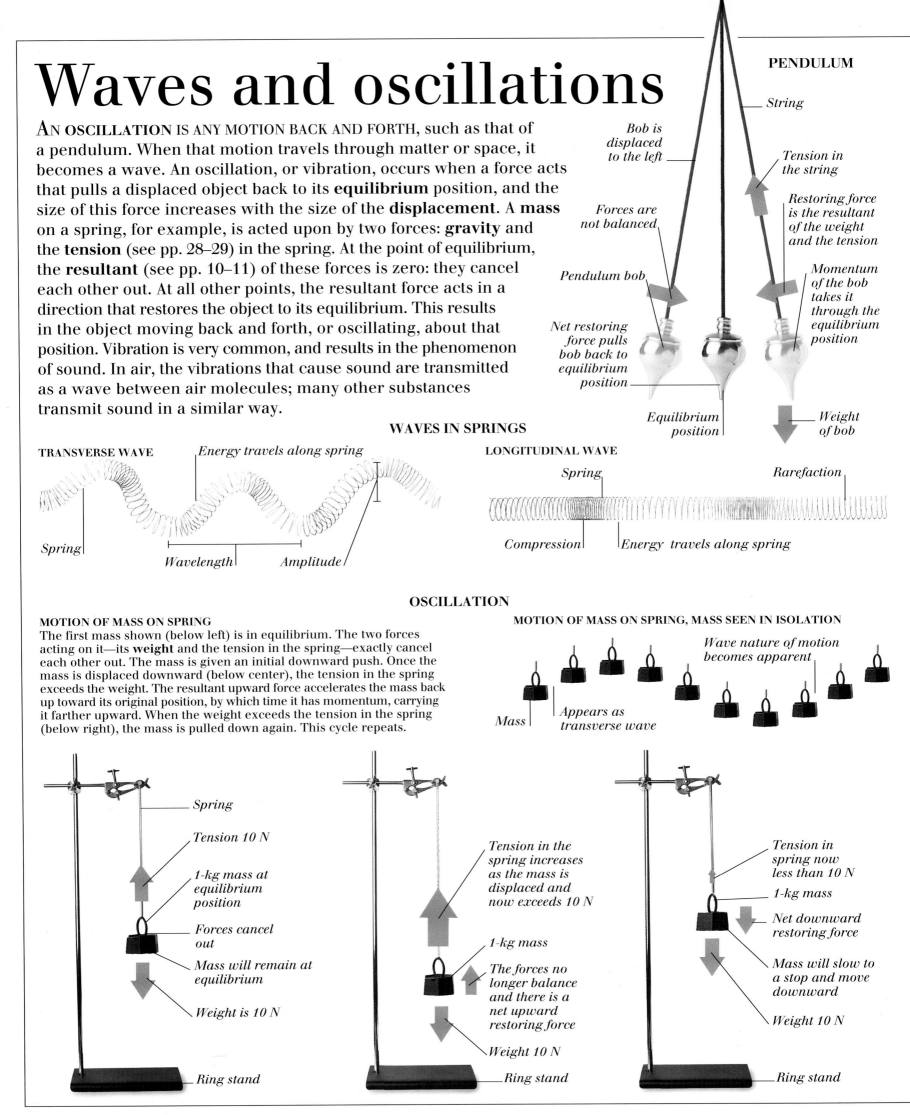

PENDULUM

- String
- Bob is displaced to the left
- Tension in the string
- Forces are not balanced
- Restoring force is the resultant of the weight and the tension
- Pendulum bob
- Momentum of the bob takes it through the equilibrium position
- Net restoring force pulls bob back to equilibrium position
- Equilibrium position
- Weight of bob

WAVES IN SPRINGS

TRANSVERSE WAVE
- Energy travels along spring
- Spring
- Wavelength
- Amplitude

LONGITUDINAL WAVE
- Spring
- Rarefaction
- Compression
- Energy travels along spring

OSCILLATION

MOTION OF MASS ON SPRING
The first mass shown (below left) is in equilibrium. The two forces acting on it—its **weight** and the tension in the spring—exactly cancel each other out. The mass is given an initial downward push. Once the mass is displaced downward (below center), the tension in the spring exceeds the weight. The resultant upward force accelerates the mass back up toward its original position, by which time it has momentum, carrying it farther upward. When the weight exceeds the tension in the spring (below right), the mass is pulled down again. This cycle repeats.

MOTION OF MASS ON SPRING, MASS SEEN IN ISOLATION
- Wave nature of motion becomes apparent
- Mass
- Appears as transverse wave

- Spring
- Tension 10 N
- 1-kg mass at equilibrium position
- Forces cancel out
- Mass will remain at equilibrium
- Weight is 10 N
- Ring stand

- Tension in the spring increases as the mass is displaced and now exceeds 10 N
- 1-kg mass
- The forces no longer balance and there is a net upward restoring force
- Weight 10 N
- Ring stand

- Tension in spring now less than 10 N
- 1-kg mass
- Net downward restoring force
- Mass will slow to a stop and move downward
- Weight 10 N
- Ring stand

SOUND AS VIBRATION OF THE AIR

PROPAGATION OF SOUND

A vibrating object, such as the tuning fork shown here, causes variations in pressure in the surrounding air. Areas of high and low **pressure**, known as **compressions** and **rarefactions**, propagate (move) through the air as sound waves. The sound waves meet a microphone, and create electrical oscillations displayed on an oscilloscope.

Low-pressure area
(rarefaction)

High-pressure area
(compression)

The compression travels
as a wave at about
330 meters
per second

Air molecules
closer than
usual

Tuning fork
produces
sound

Sound
wave

COMPRESSION

Microphone produces
electrical oscillations

Cable takes
electrical signal
to oscilloscope

Wave has a
frequency
of 440 Hz

Pressure variations
move outward
from tuning fork

Wavelength

Screen
displays
electrical
signal

Prongs of
fork vibrate
at 440 times
each second

Air molecules
farther apart
than usual

Compressions and
rarefactions reach
the microphone

Tuning fork
rated at 440
hertz (Hz)

RAREFACTION

Oscilloscope
(cathode ray
oscilloscope)

Maximum
points of wave
correspond to
compression

Minimum
points of wave
correspond to
rarefaction

NOTES PRODUCED BY COLUMNS OF AIR

FREQUENCY AND WAVELENGTH

The distance between each compression of a sound wave is called its **wavelength**. Sound waves with a short wavelength have a high **frequency** and sound high-pitched. The frequency of a note is the number of vibrations each second, and is measured in hertz (Hz). The columns of air in these jars produce different notes when air is blown over them.

Air blown across
the top of the jar
produces sound

Large variations
in pressure

Large variations
in pressure

Half of one
wavelength

Air column
0.14-m long

Half of one
wavelength

Air column
0.28-m long

No variations
in pressure

No variations
in pressure

Sound
produced has
a frequency of
about 1,240 Hz
and sounds
high-pitched

Sound
produced has
a frequency of
about 620 Hz
and sounds
lower pitched

Colored
water

Narrow
glass jar

LOUDSPEAKER

A changing electrical signal is fed to the voice coil of a loudspeaker, which lies within the **magnetic field** of a **permanent magnet**. The signal in the coil causes it to behave like an **electromagnet** (see pp. 34–35), making it push against the field of the permanent magnet. The speaker cone is then pushed in and out by the coil in time with the signal.

If the signal is from a sound
recording the original sound
will be reproduced

Collar

Voice coil

Speaker
cone is
pushed in
and out to
produce
sound

Permanent
magnet

Terminal

21

Heat and temperature

Heat is a form of energy (see pp. 6–7). This energy is the kinetic energy of the atoms and molecules that make up all matter. The temperature of a substance is related to the average kinetic energy of its particles. Units of temperature include the degree Celsius(°C), the degree Fahrenheit (°F), and the Kelvin (K). Some examples of equivalent values are shown below. At absolute zero (zero K), particles of matter do not vibrate, but at all other temperatures, particles have some motion. The state of a substance is determined by its temperature and most substances can exist as a solid (see pp. 24–25), a liquid (see pp. 26–27), or a gas (see pp. 28–29). If two substances at different temperatures make contact, their particles will share their energy. This results in a heat transfer by conduction, until the temperatures are equal. This process can melt a solid, in which case the heat transferred is called latent heat. Heat can also be transferred by radiation, in which heat energy becomes electromagnetic radiation (see pp. 38–39), and does not need a material medium to transfer heat.

RANGE OF TEMPERATURES

About 14 million K (14 million °C, 25 million °F): Center of the Sun

30,000K (30,000°C, 54,000°F): Average bolt of lightning

5,800K (5,530°C, 10,000°F): Surface of the Sun

3,300K (3,027°C; 5,480°F): Metals can be welded

1,808K (1,535°C, 2,795°F): Melting point of iron

933K (660°C, 1,220°F): Natural gas flame

600K (327°C, 620°F): Melting point of lead

523K (250°C, 482°F): Wood burns

457K (184°C, 363°F): Paper ignites

373.15K (100°C, 212°F): Boiling point of water

331K (58°C, 136°F): Earth's highest temperature

273.15K (0°C, 32°F): Freezing point of water

234K (-39°C, -38.2°F): Freezing point of mercury

184K (-89°C, -128°F): Earth's lowest temperature

73K (-200°C, -328°F): Air liquifies

0K (-273.15°C, -459.67°F): Absolute zero

TEMPERATURE SCALES

All temperature scales except the Kelvin scale (K) need two or more reference temperatures, such as boiling water and melting ice. Under controlled conditions, these two temperatures are fixed.

STATES OF MATTER

GAS

Heat energy applied to a liquid allows particles to become free of each other and become a gas. However if enough energy is removed from a gas, by cooling, it condenses to a liquid.

SUPERCOOLED LIQUID

The particles of a **supercooled liquid** are in fixed positions, like those of a solid, but they are disordered and cannot be called a true solid. Supercooled liquids flow like liquids, but very slowly, and they have no definite melting point.

GAS

Sublimation (solid to gas or gas to solid)

Evaporation (liquid to gas)

Condensation (gas to liquid)

Supercooling (liquid to glass)

Crystallization (glass to solid)

SUPERCOOLED LIQUID

SOLID

The particles of a solid normally have no motion relative to each other, as they are only free to vibrate about a fixed position. An input of energy breaks the bonds between particles, and the solid melts.

SOLID MATTER

Freezing (liquid to solid)

Melting (solid or glass to liquid)

LIQUID

LIQUID

Particles in a liquid do not occupy fixed positions like those in a solid, but neither are they completely free, as in a gas. The particles move over one another, allowing a liquid to flow.

EQUALIZATION OF TEMPERATURES

OBJECTS AT DIFFERENT TEMPERATURES
The particles of objects at different temperatures have different kinetic energies. The colors of the blocks below are an indication of their temperature.

TRANSFER OF HEAT
When two objects at different temperatures are brought into contact, a transfer of kinetic energy—in the form of heat—takes place. Here, the hot and cold blocks are touching.

EQUAL TEMPERATURES
Eventually, the average kinetic energies of particles in two touching objects become equal. The temperatures of the two objects are then said to be equal, as shown by the blocks below.

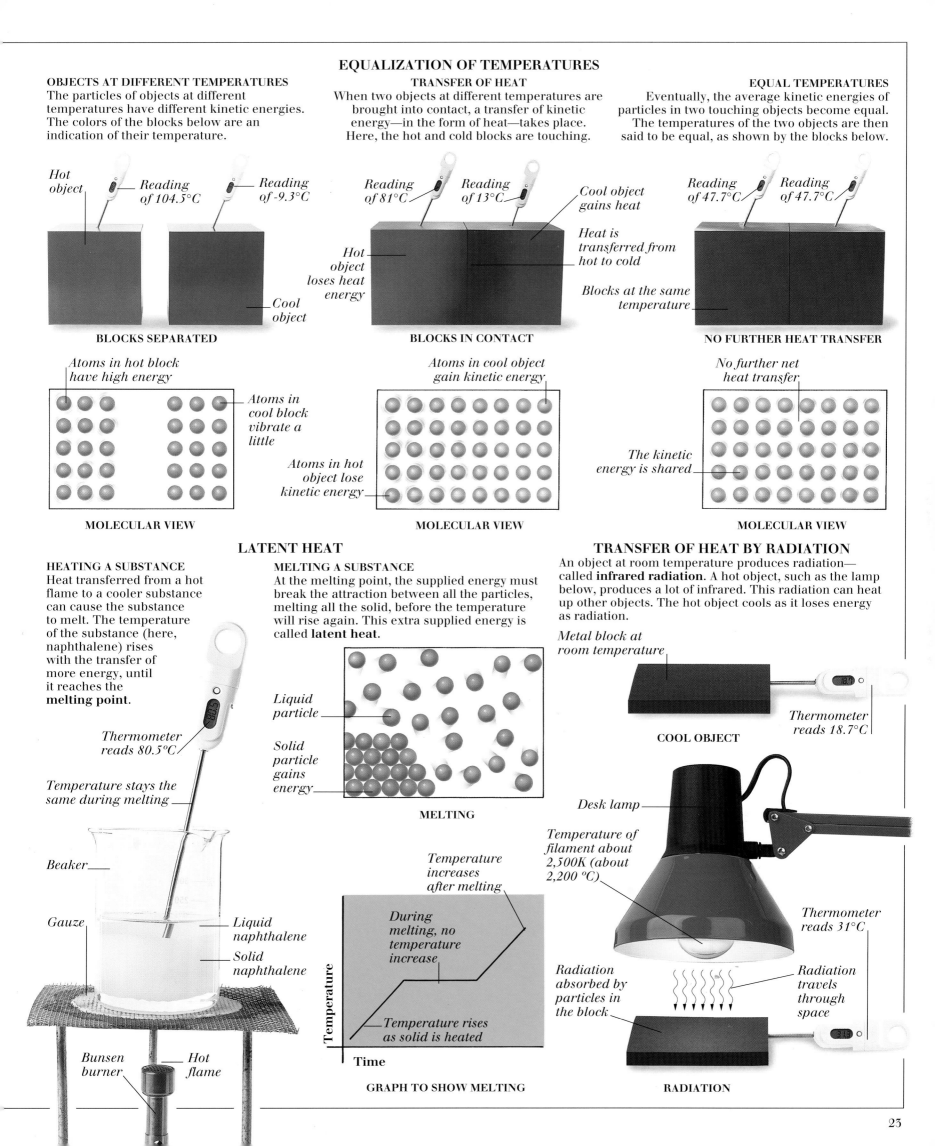

Hot object

Reading of 104.5°C

Reading of -9.3°C

Cool object

BLOCKS SEPARATED

Reading of 81°C

Reading of 13°C

Cool object gains heat

Hot object loses heat energy

Heat is transferred from hot to cold

BLOCKS IN CONTACT

Reading of 47.7°C

Reading of 47.7°C

Blocks at the same temperature

NO FURTHER HEAT TRANSFER

Atoms in hot block have high energy

Atoms in cool block vibrate a little

MOLECULAR VIEW

Atoms in cool object gain kinetic energy

Atoms in hot object lose kinetic energy

MOLECULAR VIEW

No further net heat transfer

The kinetic energy is shared

MOLECULAR VIEW

LATENT HEAT

HEATING A SUBSTANCE
Heat transferred from a hot flame to a cooler substance can cause the substance to melt. The temperature of the substance (here, naphthalene) rises with the transfer of more energy, until it reaches the **melting point**.

Thermometer reads 80.5°C

Temperature stays the same during melting

Beaker

Gauze

Liquid naphthalene

Solid naphthalene

Bunsen burner

Hot flame

MELTING A SUBSTANCE
At the melting point, the supplied energy must break the attraction between all the particles, melting all the solid, before the temperature will rise again. This extra supplied energy is called **latent heat**.

Liquid particle

Solid particle gains energy

MELTING

Temperature increases after melting

During melting, no temperature increase

Temperature rises as solid is heated

Temperature

Time

GRAPH TO SHOW MELTING

TRANSFER OF HEAT BY RADIATION
An object at room temperature produces radiation—called **infrared radiation**. A hot object, such as the lamp below, produces a lot of infrared. This radiation can heat up other objects. The hot object cools as it loses energy as radiation.

Metal block at room temperature

Thermometer reads 18.7°C

COOL OBJECT

Desk lamp

Temperature of filament about 2,500K (about 2,200 °C)

Thermometer reads 31°C

Radiation absorbed by particles in the block

Radiation travels through space

RADIATION

Solids

THE ATOMS OF A SOLID ARE CLOSELY PACKED, giving it a greater **density** than most liquids, and all gases. A solid's rigidity derives from the strong attraction between its atoms. A force pulling on a solid moves these atoms farther apart, creating an opposing force called **tension**. If a force pushes on a solid, the atoms move closer together, creating **compression**. Temperature (see pp. 22–23) can also affect the nature of a solid. When the temperature of a solid increases, its particles gain **kinetic energy** and vibrate more vigorously, resulting in **thermal expansion**. Most solids are **crystals**, in which atoms are arranged in one of seven regular, repeating patterns (see below). **Amorphous solids**, such as glass, are not composed of crystals and can be molded into any shape. When the atoms of a solid move apart, the length of the solid increases. The extent of this increase depends on the applied force and the thickness of the material, and is known as **elasticity**.

STEEL RAILS
The expansion of a solid with an increase in temperature (see below) would cause rails to buckle badly in hot weather. To prevent this, rails are made in sections. The gap between the two sections allows each section to expand without buckling.

Train can pass smoothly over diagonal joint

Expansion joint

THERMAL EXPANSION

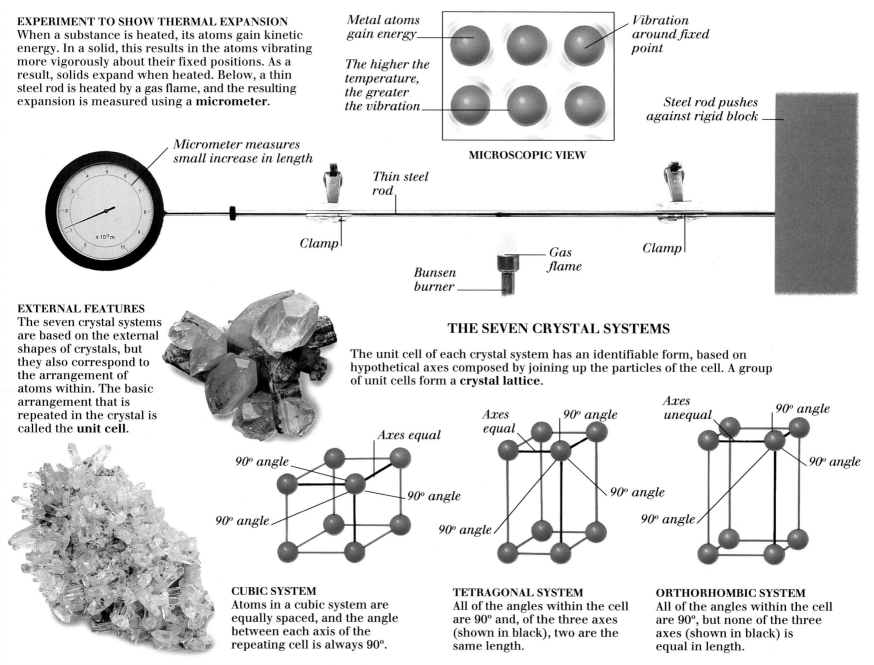

EXPERIMENT TO SHOW THERMAL EXPANSION
When a substance is heated, its atoms gain kinetic energy. In a solid, this results in the atoms vibrating more vigorously about their fixed positions. As a result, solids expand when heated. Below, a thin steel rod is heated by a gas flame, and the resulting expansion is measured using a **micrometer**.

Metal atoms gain energy

The higher the temperature, the greater the vibration

Vibration around fixed point

MICROSCOPIC VIEW

Steel rod pushes against rigid block

Micrometer measures small increase in length

Thin steel rod

Clamp

Bunsen burner

Gas flame

Clamp

EXTERNAL FEATURES
The seven crystal systems are based on the external shapes of crystals, but they also correspond to the arrangement of atoms within. The basic arrangement that is repeated in the crystal is called the **unit cell**.

THE SEVEN CRYSTAL SYSTEMS

The unit cell of each crystal system has an identifiable form, based on hypothetical axes composed by joining up the particles of the cell. A group of unit cells form a **crystal lattice**.

Axes equal

90° angle

90° angle

90° angle

90° angle

CUBIC SYSTEM
Atoms in a cubic system are equally spaced, and the angle between each axis of the repeating cell is always 90°.

Axes equal

90° angle

90° angle

90° angle

TETRAGONAL SYSTEM
All of the angles within the cell are 90° and, of the three axes (shown in black), two are the same length.

Axes unequal

90° angle

90° angle

90° angle

90° angle

ORTHORHOMBIC SYSTEM
All of the angles within the cell are 90°, but none of the three axes (shown in black) is equal in length.

Hook

Wooden support

ATOMS IN UNEXTENDED RUBBER

ATOMS IN RUBBER UNDER TENSION

ATOMS UNDER GREATER TENSION

Thick rubber strip

Strip is twice as thick as thin strip

Rubber strip

Length of strip 15 cm

Atoms in rubber move apart

Bonds between atoms extend

Bonds between atoms extend farther

Atoms in rubber move apart

Rubber strip now has length of 17 cm

Line showing original length of rubber strip

Rubber strip now has length of 19 cm

Much larger force would break bonds

Rubber strip now has length of 17 cm

Rubber strip now has length of 17 cm

Extension of rubber 2 cm

Extension 2 cm

2-kg mass (weight 20 N)

Much larger force would break the material

Extension of rubber 4 cm

EXPERIMENT TO TEST ELASTICITY
An elastic substance is a solid that gets larger (extends) under tension, gets smaller under compression, and returns to its original size when no force acts on it. All nonamorphous solids are to a certain extent elastic. This experiment, which tests rubber under different degrees of tension, shows that twice the tension force results in twice the extension.

1-kg mass (weight 10 N)

2-kg mass (weight 20 N)

CROSS-SECTIONAL AREA
Another factor involved in elasticity is the cross-sectional area of the material involved. The thick rubber strip (above) extends less under the same tension than the thinner one (above left).

Axes unequal

90° angle

120° angle

90° angle

Two axes equal

All three angles different

All axes equal

No axes equal

No angles equal

MONOCLINIC SYSTEM
Two of the axes of the cell meet at 90°. No two axes (shown in black) are equal in length.

HEXAGONAL SYSTEM
The edges form angles of 120° and 90°. Two of the three axes (shown in black) are equal in length.

TRIGONAL SYSTEM
No two edges meet at 90°. All of the edges are equal in length.

TRICLINIC SYSTEM
No two edges meet at 90°. No two axes (shown in black) are equal in length.

Liquids

UNLIKE SOLIDS, LIQUIDS CAN FLOW. Their particles move almost independently of each other but are not as free as the particles of a gas. Forces of attraction called **cohesive** forces act between the particles of a liquid. These forces create **surface tension**, which pulls liquid drops into a spherical shape. If the surface tension of water is reduced by dissolving soap in it, then pockets of air can stretch the surface into a thin film, forming a bubble. Forces of attraction between liquid particles and adjoining matter are called **adhesive** forces. The balance between cohesive and adhesive forces causes **capillary action**, and the formation of a **meniscus** curve at the boundary between a liquid and its container. Liquids exert pressure on any object immersed in them; the pressure acts in all directions and increases with depth, creating **upthrust** on an immersed object. If the upthrust is large enough, the object will float.

LIQUID DROPS AND BUBBLES

COHESIVE FORCES
No **resultant** force acts on any particle within the liquid, because cohesive forces pull it in every direction. But at the surface, the resultant force on each particle pulls it inward. This causes surface tension, which pulls drops and bubbles into spheres. A water drop on a surface will be flattened slightly by gravity.

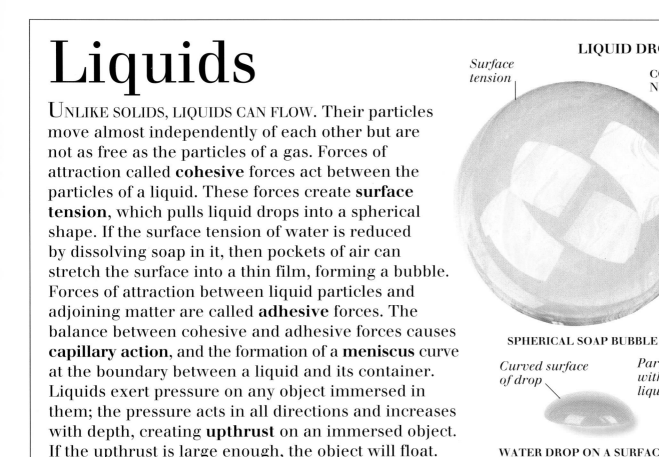

Surface tension

SPHERICAL SOAP BUBBLE

Curved surface of drop

WATER DROP ON A SURFACE

Cohesive forces act in all directions *Curved surface of drop* *Surface particle*

Particle within liquid

SURFACE TENSION

LIQUIDS IN TUBES

CAPILLARY ACTION
Water adheres to glass. This adhesion can lift water up into a glass tube; an effect known as capillary action.

Narrow 0.5-mm capillary tube

4-mm diameter glass tube

5-mm diameter glass tube

Water level

Water is lifted higher in a narrow tube than in a wide one because the narrow column of water weighs less

Water level

Water level

Shallow glass dish

Body of liquid

MENISCUS
Where a liquid meets a solid surface, a curve called a meniscus forms. The shape of the meniscus depends on the balance between cohesive and adhesive forces.

DOWNWARD MENISCUS

Narrow tube

Glass

Downward meniscus forms because adhesion is stronger than cohesion

Water drop

MOLECULAR VIEW
Capillary action is caused by adhesive and cohesive forces between particles of glass and water. Here, water molecules adhere to glass and the adhesive force lifts the edge of the water up the glass. The cohesive forces between water molecules means that this lifted edge also raises water molecules lying farther out from the edge of the glass.

Wall of glass tube

Molecules of the glass

Water is pulled upward by adhesive forces

Water molecules

Cohesive forces pull other water molecules up

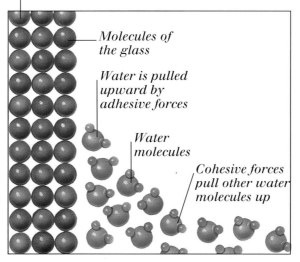

UPWARD MENISCUS

Narrow tube

Glass

Upward meniscus forms because cohesion is stronger than adhesion

Drop of mercury

UPTHRUST ON IMMERSED OBJECTS

Liquids exert **pressure** on immersed objects, resulting in an upward resultant force called upthrust. The upthrust is equal to the **weight** of liquid displaced by the immersed object. Here, a 1-kg mass, weighing 10 N in air, displaces water weighing 1.2 N. Consequently the apparent weight of the submerged mass is 8.8 N (10 N – 1.2 N).

10-N reading

Newton meter

1-kg mass

Water displaced by immersed object

Pan

Weight of water 1.2 N

Scale graded in newtons

Newton meter

8.8-N reading

Water level rises as object is immersed

1-kg mass

Water

OBJECT SUSPENDED IN AIR

OBJECT IMMERSED IN WATER

UPTHRUST AT WORK

If the upthrust on an object is greater than the weight of the object, then the object will float. Large metal ships float, because their shape means that they displace huge amounts of water, producing a large upthrust.

Metal hull

Upthrust force from the water equals the downward force of the ship's weight

THE WATER JETS

The water in the jets coming from the tank breaks into drops as it falls. Surface tension pulls the water into drops as the jet weakens and cohesive forces keep the drops in a near spherical shape. When the drops fall into the tray, they form a pool. Unlike solids, liquids can flow, so under the influence of **gravity** the surface of this pool becomes flat and horizontal.

Shallow tray

Flat and horizontal surface

Colored water

PRESSURE INCREASES WITH DEPTH

The pressure at any point in a liquid depends on the weight of liquid above that point. So pressure increases with depth. In the experiment shown below, water from a large tank escapes through holes at various depths. The greater the pressure, the faster the water escapes.

The pressure of a liquid is measured in newtons per square meter (Nm^{-2})

Atmospheric pressure above the water's surface is 100,000 Nm^{-2}

Pressure gauge

Clear plastic tank

Pressure at 0.1-m depth is 101,000 Nm^{-2}

Only a dribble of water escapes

Water escapes quickly

Pressure at 0.2-m depth is 102,000 Nm^{-2}

Pressure at 0.3-m depth is 103,000 Nm^{-2}

Stream is almost horizontal

Water escapes very quickly

Colored water

Water pressure greatest at the base of the tank

Gases

A GAS COMPRISES INDEPENDENT PARTICLES—**atoms** or **molecules**—in random motion. This means that a gas will fill any container into which it is placed. If two different gases are allowed to meet, the particles of the gases will mix together. This process is known as **diffusion**. Imagine a fixed mass of gas—that is, a fixed number of gas particles. It will occupy a particular amount of space, or **volume**, often confined by a container. The particles of the gas will be in constant, random motion. The higher the **temperature** of the gas (see pp. 22–23), the faster the particles move. The bombardment of particles against the sides of the container produces **pressure** (see pp. 10–11). Three simple laws describe the predictable behavior of gases. They are Boyle's Law, the Pressure Law, and Charles' Law. Each of the gas laws describes a relationship between the pressure, volume, and temperature of a gas.

Clear plexiglass shield

Closed glass tube

Thick tube wall withstands pressure

Volume of trapped air

Column of oil

After each pressure change, apparatus is allowed to revert to room temperature

BOYLE'S LAW
The volume of a **mass** of gas at a fixed temperature will change in relation to the pressure. If the pressure on a gas increases, its volume will decrease. The apparatus on the left is used to illustrate Boyle's Law. A foot pump is used to push a column of oil up a sealed tube, reducing the volume occupied by the gas in the top part of the tube.

DIFFUSION
The random movement of gas particles ensures that any two gases sharing the same container will totally mix. This is diffusion. In the experiment below, the lower gas jar contains bromine, the top one air.

Random motion leads to random mixing of the molecules

Air

Slip separating air from bromine removed

Some air moves into the bromine and mixes with it

Bromine gas

Random motion of the molecules leads to the complete mixing of air and bromine

Some bromine moves into the air and mixes with it

Pressure is measured at various volumes and the results are shown as a graph

Bourdon gauge measures pressure

GRAPH OF PRESSURE AND VOLUME READINGS

Doubling the pressure halves the volume

Volume (m^{-3}) / Pressure (x 1,000 Nm^{-2})

Rubber tubing

Foot pump

Base

Connecting pipe

PRESSURE LAW

The pressure exerted by a gas at constant volume increases as the temperature of the gas rises. The apparatus shown is used to verify the Pressure Law. A mass of gas is heated in a water bath, and the pressure of the gas measured. When plotted as points on a graph the results lie on a straight line.

Thermometer measures temperature of the water bath

Clamp

Glass tubing

Doubling the temperature doubles the pressure

GRAPH OF PRESSURE AND TEMPERATURE READINGS

Pressure (x 10⁵ Nm⁻²)

120
115
110
105
100

300 310 320 340 360

Temperature (K)

Spherical flask

Glass beaker

Wire mesh

Bunsen burner

Tripod

Temperature of gas is the same as that of water bath

Bourdon gauge measures gas pressure

CHARLES' LAW

The volume of a mass of gas at a fixed pressure depends on its temperature. The higher the temperature, the greater the volume. The apparatus shown is used to illustrate Charles' Law. The volume of a gas sample in the glass bulb is noted at various temperatures. A graph shows the results.

Opening clip keeps pressure of gas sample constant

Reservoir tube can be used to supply gas other than air

Clamp

Water stirrer ensures water is at an even temperature

Thermometer

Volume of gas measured against scale

Glass sphere enclosing gas sample

Water

Glass beaker

Wire mesh

Tripod

Bunsen burner

GRAPH OF TEMPERATURE AND VOLUME READINGS

Doubling the temperature doubles the volume

Volume (cm³)

34
32
30
28

290 300 310 320 330 340 350

Temperature (K)

HOT AIR BALLOON – CHARLES' LAW IN ACTION

The air in the envelope of a hot air balloon is heated by a gas burner. As its temperature rises, the gas expands in accordance with Charles' Law. The envelope is open at the bottom, so some hot air escapes. Because air has mass (and therefore **weight**), the balloon weighs less once some air has escaped, although its volume is still large. The pressure of the air outside the envelope produces an **upthrust,** which, if enough air has been lost from the envelope, will be great enough to lift the balloon.

Envelope

Hot air escapes

Gas burner

Basket

Electricity and magnetism

ALL ELECTRICAL EFFECTS ARE CAUSED by **electric charges**. There are two types of electric charge, positive and negative. These charges exert **electrostatic** forces on each other. An **electric field** is the region in which these forces have effect. In atoms, **protons** (see pp. 48–49) carry positive charge, while **electrons** carry negative charge. **Atoms** are normally neutral, having equal numbers of each charge, but an atom can gain or lose electrons, for example by being rubbed. It then becomes a charged atom, or **ion**. Ions can be produced continuously by a Van de Graaff generator. Ions in a charged object may cause another nearby object to become charged. This process is called **induction**. Electricity has many similarities with magnetism (see pp. 34–35). For example, the lines of the electric field between charges (see right) take the same form as lines of magnetic force (see opposite), so magnetic fields are equivalent to electric fields. Iron consists of small magnetized regions called **domains**. If the magnetic directions of the domains in a piece of iron line up, the iron becomes magnetized.

ELECTRIC FIELDS AND FORCES

Charges of the same type repel, while charges of a different type attract. One way to think of an electric field is as a set of lines of force, as illustrated below.

Lines of force

Charges attract each other

TWO SIMILAR CHARGES

Electric field

Lines of force

TWO DIFFERENT CHARGES

Charges repel each other

STATIC ELECTRICITY

GOLD LEAF ELECTROSCOPE

A polyethylene rod can gain extra electrons when it is rubbed. Touching the charged rod to the top of an electroscope causes electrons to move into the electroscope. The electrons in the central strip and in the gold leaf repel each other, and the leaf lifts.

INDUCTION

When a charged object is brought near to other materials, such as paper, electrostatic forces cause a displacement of charge within that material. This is called induction. Negative charges in the paper are displaced so the edge of the paper nearest the rod becomes positively charged and clings to the negatively charged rod.

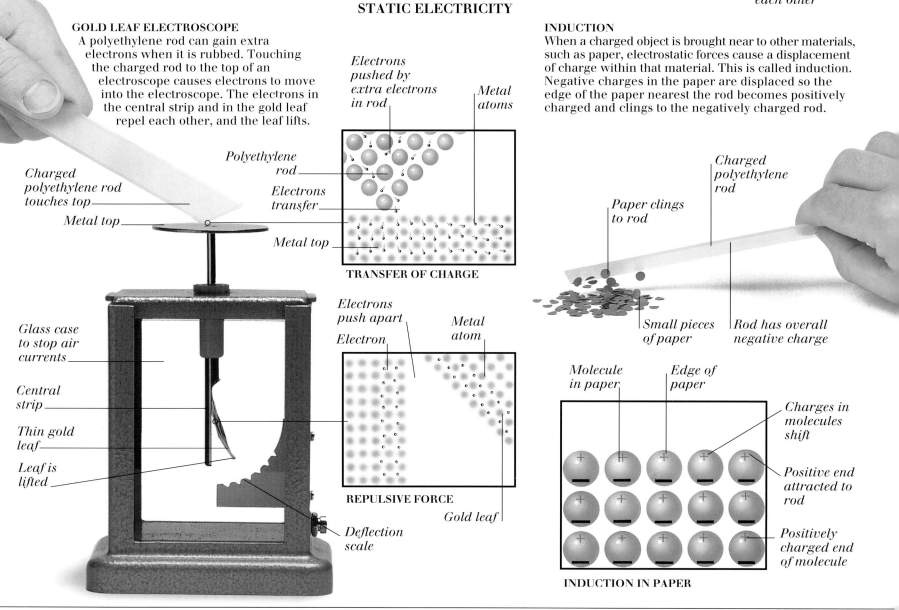

Charged polyethylene rod touches top

Metal top

Electrons pushed by extra electrons in rod

Metal atoms

Polyethylene rod

Electrons transfer

Metal top

TRANSFER OF CHARGE

Glass case to stop air currents

Central strip

Thin gold leaf

Leaf is lifted

Electrons push apart

Electron

Metal atom

Gold leaf

REPULSIVE FORCE

Deflection scale

Charged polyethylene rod

Paper clings to rod

Small pieces of paper

Rod has overall negative charge

Molecule in paper

Edge of paper

Charges in molecules shift

Positive end attracted to rod

Positively charged end of molecule

INDUCTION IN PAPER

VAN DE GRAAFF GENERATOR

Metal dome

Voltage of tens of thousands of volts

Plastic support for dome

Belt driven by electric motor

Electrons jump from metal objects neutralizing positive ions in the dome, appearing as a spark

Metal object brought near dome

Metal support

Base unit containing motor

GENERATION OF IONS
A Van de Graaff generator separates electrons from the atoms of a moving belt. The positive ions created are carried upward by the belt, and take electrons from atoms of a metal dome. The electric field around the dome becomes very strong.

Millions of positive ions

Rotation of belt

Metal dome

Positively charged belt strips negative charges (electrons) from dome via metal comb, giving dome a positive charge

Pulley wheel

Insulating column prevents charge from leaking away

Moving rubber belt gains a positive charge

Positive metal comb strips negative charges (electrons) from belt

Negatively charged metal plate

Connection to positive electrical supply

Pulley wheel

Connection to negative electrical supply

Rotation of belt

MAGNETISM

MAGNETIC COMPASS
Walkers and sailors use magnetic compasses to find their way. The needle of a compass lines up with the Earth's magnetic field, and always points North-South. The Earth's magnetism is thought to be caused by currents in its molten iron core.

Needle is a small magnet that is free to turn

Needle is suspended in fluid

Bearing readings are taken from this scale

MAGNETIC FIELDS AND FORCES

Iron filings

Profile of magnetic field

South-seeking pole

North-seeking pole

Every magnet has two ends or poles

Bar magnet

North-seeking pole

Like poles repel

North-seeking pole

Opposite poles attract

South-seeking pole

MAGNET DOMAINS

Direction of magnetization within domain is random

Domain

Domain boundary

Direction of magnetization within domain has aligned

Domain aligned with magnetization has grown

Domain not aligned with magnetization has shrunk

Direction of overall magnetization

UNMAGNETIZED IRON

MAGNETIZED IRON

Electric circuits

AN ELECTRIC CIRCUIT IS SIMPLY THE COURSE along which an **electric current** flows. **Electrons** carry negative charge and can be moved around a circuit by **electrostatic forces** (see pp. 30–31). A circuit usually consists of a **conductive** material, such as a metal, where the electrons are held very loosely to their atoms, thus making movement possible. The strength of the electrostatic force is the **voltage,** and is measured in volts (V). The resulting movement of electric charge is called an electric current, and is measured in amps (A). The higher the voltage, the greater the current will be. But the current also depends on the thickness, length, temperature, and nature of the material that conducts it. The **resistance** of a material is the extent to which it opposes the flow of electric current, and is measured in ohms (Ω). Good conductors have a low resistance, which means that a small voltage will produce a large current. In batteries, the dissolving of a metal **electrode** causes the freeing of electrons, resulting in their movement to another electrode and the formation of a current.

ELECTRIC CURRENT

Regions of positive or negative charge, such as those at the terminals of a battery, force electrons through a conductor. The electrons move from negative charge toward positive. Originally, current was thought to flow from positive to negative. This is called "conventional current."

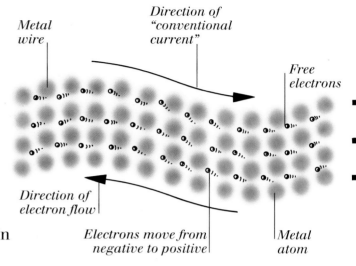

Metal wire

Direction of "conventional current"

Free electrons

Direction of electron flow

Electrons move from negative to positive

Metal atom

RESISTANCE

OHM'S LAW

A thin wire has a resistance to the flow of current. The longer and thinner the wire, the higher the resistance. An object's resistance can be worked out by dividing the voltage by the current (see p. 54).

Voltmeter measures voltage

Ammeter measures current

Banana plug

Clip

Cell

Voltage across wire: 0.99 V

Current through wire: 1.21 A

Long, thin wire made of nichrome

Resistance of wire: 0.82 Ω

Thick connecting wires have little resistance

Current flowing through resistor: 0.18 A

Ammeter

Connecting wire

22 Ω RESISTANCE

Electrical components called resistors allow current in circuits to be controlled. The current flowing around a circuit can be worked out using Ohm's Law.

Negative terminal

Positive terminal

22 Ω resistor

4.5 V battery

Ammeter

47 Ω RESISTANCE

The larger the resistor, the smaller the current. The smaller the resistor, the larger the current.

Current flowing through resistor: 0.09 A

Negative terminal

Positive terminal

4.5 V battery

47 Ω resistor

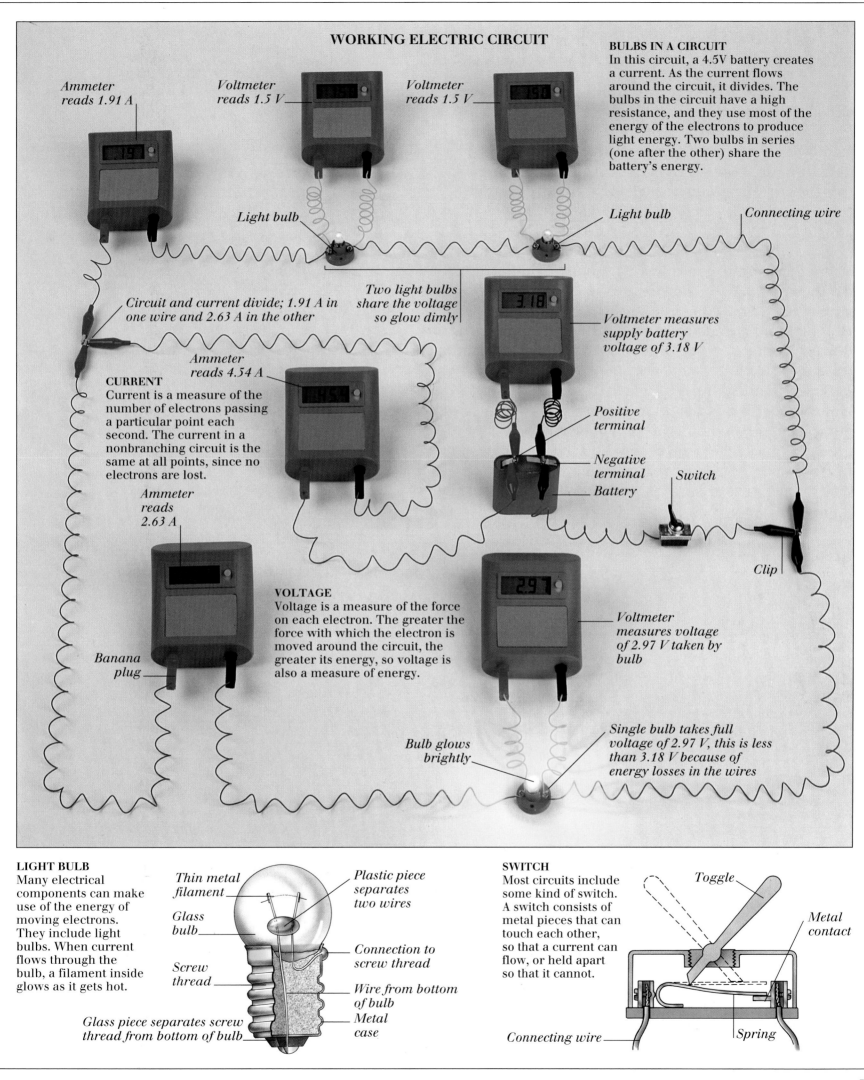

WORKING ELECTRIC CIRCUIT

Ammeter reads 1.91 A

Voltmeter reads 1.5 V

Voltmeter reads 1.5 V

BULBS IN A CIRCUIT
In this circuit, a 4.5V battery creates a current. As the current flows around the circuit, it divides. The bulbs in the circuit have a high resistance, and they use most of the energy of the electrons to produce light energy. Two bulbs in series (one after the other) share the battery's energy.

Light bulb

Light bulb

Connecting wire

Circuit and current divide; 1.91 A in one wire and 2.63 A in the other

Two light bulbs share the voltage so glow dimly

Voltmeter measures supply battery voltage of 3.18 V

Ammeter reads 4.54 A

CURRENT
Current is a measure of the number of electrons passing a particular point each second. The current in a nonbranching circuit is the same at all points, since no electrons are lost.

Positive terminal

Negative terminal

Battery

Switch

Ammeter reads 2.63 A

Clip

VOLTAGE
Voltage is a measure of the force on each electron. The greater the force with which the electron is moved around the circuit, the greater its energy, so voltage is also a measure of energy.

Voltmeter measures voltage of 2.97 V taken by bulb

Banana plug

Single bulb takes full voltage of 2.97 V, this is less than 3.18 V because of energy losses in the wires

Bulb glows brightly

LIGHT BULB
Many electrical components can make use of the energy of moving electrons. They include light bulbs. When current flows through the bulb, a filament inside glows as it gets hot.

Thin metal filament

Plastic piece separates two wires

Glass bulb

Screw thread

Connection to screw thread

Wire from bottom of bulb

Metal case

Glass piece separates screw thread from bottom of bulb

SWITCH
Most circuits include some kind of switch. A switch consists of metal pieces that can touch each other, so that a current can flow, or held apart so that it cannot.

Toggle

Metal contact

Connecting wire

Spring

Electromagnetism

ANY ELECTRIC CURRENT WILL PRODUCE magnetism that affects iron filings and a compass needle in the same way as an ordinary, "permanent" magnet. The arrangement of "force lines" around a wire carrying an electric current— its **magnetic field**—is circular. The magnetic effect of electric current is increased by making the current-carrying wire into a coil. When a coil is wrapped around an iron bar, it is called an **electromagnet**. The magnetic field produced by the coil magnetizes the iron bar, strengthening the overall effect. A field like that of a bar magnet (see p. 31) is formed by the magnetic fields of the wires in the coil. The strength of the magnetism produced depends on the number of coils and the size of the current flowing in the wires. A huge number of machines and appliances exploit the connection between electricity and magnetism, including electric motors. Electromagnetic coils and permanent magnets are arranged inside an electric motor so that the forces of electromagnetism create rotation of a central spindle. This principle can be used on a large scale to generate immense forces.

MAGNETIC FIELD AROUND A CURRENT-CARRYING WIRE

The magnetic field produced by a current in a single wire is circular. Here, iron filings sprinkled around a current-carrying wire are made to line up by the magnetic field.

No current flowing through wire   *White card*   *Iron filings*

NO CURRENT THROUGH WIRE

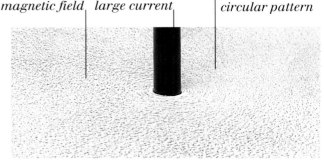

Circular magnetic field   *Wire carrying large current*   *Each piece of iron lines up with the field to form a circular pattern*

CURRENT THROUGH WIRE

ELECTROMAGNETISM AFFECTING A COMPASS NEEDLE

A compass needle is a small magnet that is free to swivel around. It normally points north-south, in line with the Earth's magnetic field. But when a current flows in an adjacent wire, the needle swings around to line up with the field created by the current.

NO CURRENT, NO MAGNETIC FIELD

Ammeter shows that there is no current flowing in circuit

No current flowing

4.5 V battery

No current flows in wire

Variable resistor clicked off to prevent flow of current

Clip

Compass needle points north-south

Compass

CURRENT FLOWING, MAGNETIC FIELD PRODUCED

Ammeter shows that current is flowing

4.5V battery

Variable resistor adjusted to allow current to flow

Current flows in wire

Compass

Compass needle aligns with magnetic field produced by current

Current produces magnetic field

ELECTROMAGNETS

THE STRENGTH OF AN ELECTROMAGNET
An electromagnet is a coil of wire wrapped around an iron bar. It behaves like a permanent magnet, except that it can be turned off. Here, the size of the magnetic force produced by an electromagnet is measured by the number of paper clips it can lift. The strength of an electromagnet depends on the number of turns in the coil and the current flowing through the wire.

Ring stand

Field produced by coil magnetizes iron bar

Clamp

Wire to battery

Clip

Coil of 50 turns

About 15 paper clips cling to electromagnet

SCRAPYARD ELECTROMAGNET

An electromagnetic crane picks up scrap metal using a powerful electromagnet. The electromagnet is switched on, scrap metal containing iron clings to it, and can be moved around. The metal is dropped by switching the magnet off.

4.5 V battery

Clip

Battery, electromagnet, and wires make a circuit

Ring stand base

A SOLENOID
The magnetic field around a coil of current-carrying wire resembles that around an ordinary bar magnet. The fields of each individual wire add up to give the overall pattern. A coil like this, with no iron bar at its core, is called a **solenoid**.

Direction of magnetic field (from north pole to south pole)

Electric current produces magnetic field

Magnetic field

Coil carries electric current

Direction of current

Metal wire (conductor) coated with plastic (insulator)

Positive terminal

Negative terminal

Four 1.5-volt cells (total of 6 volts)

Coil of 50 turns

Coil of 100 turns

Holds 30 paper clips

Holds 30 paper clips

Two 4.5 V batteries connected together to produce twice the current

4.5V battery

EFFECT OF DOUBLING CURRENT

EFFECT OF DOUBLING NUMBER OF TURNS ON COIL

ELECTRIC MOTORS
Inside the motor, an electric current is sent through a series of wire coils one by one, providing a magnetic field around each coil, one after the other. The magnetism of the coils interacts with the magnetic fields of permanent magnets placed around them. The push and pull of this interaction turns the motor. As the rotor turns, a new coil is activated and the motion continues.

Steel casing

Iron core

Coated copper wire

Commutator makes contact to each coil in turn

Permanent magnet

Terminal

Spindle

Generating electricity

THERE ARE MANY WAYS TO GENERATE electricity. The most common is to use coils of wire and magnets in a **generator**. Whenever a wire and magnet are moved relative to each other, a **voltage** is produced. In a generator, the wire is wound into a coil. The more turns in the coil and the faster the coil moves, the greater the voltage. The coils or magnets spin around at high speed, turned by water pressure, the wind, or, most commonly, by steam pressure. The steam is usually generated by burning coal or oil, a process that creates pollution. Renewable sources of electricity—such as hydroelectric power, wind power, solar energy, and geothermal power—produce only heat as pollution. In a generator, the **kinetic energy** of a spinning object is converted into electrical energy. A solar cell converts the energy of sunlight directly into electrical energy, using layers of **semiconductors**.

GENERATOR

Inside a generator, you will find coils of wire and magnets (or electromagnets). In the generator shown, electromagnets spin rapidly inside stationary coils of wire. A voltage is then produced in the coils.

An electric current will flow if the terminal is connected to a circuit

Terminal box

Main rotor turns in magnetic field produced by coil of wire in stator

Fan

Drive end

Shaft

Bearing housing

Non-drive end

Secondary (exciter) rotor

Coil of wire

HYDROELECTRIC POWER STATION
Water flows into a hydroelectric power station from a reservoir above. The water exerts pressure on **turbines** within the power station. The pressure pushes the water through the turbines, turning them at great speed. The turbine runs a generator, which produces the electricity.

WATER POWER

Transformer

Switch gear including circuit breaker

Gate

Screen

Potential energy of water admitted turns turbine

Water builds up in reservoir and flows through turbines

Penstock

Draft tube

Insulator

High voltage cable

Rotor house

Generator unit

Generator rotor turned by turbine

Shaft

Francis turbine

Gate

Curved blade

Afterbay

Tailrace

Water that flows out has lost some energy

WIND POWER

WIND TURBINE
Energy from the wind is converted to electricity by wind turbines. The rotating turbine blades are connected to a generator, which produces a voltage. The faster the wind blows and the larger the blades, the greater the energy available.

Lightning conductor

Hut

Generator

Hut can be rotated into the wind

Gears increase or decrease speed of rotation

Turbine blade

Turbine shaft

Tower

WIND FARM

Large numbers of turbines stand together in a wind farm

OTHER SOURCES
Two further examples of renewable sources are tidal power and geothermal power. The tides are a result of the gravitational pull of the Moon. Geothermal heat is produced by the disintegration of radioactive atoms in the Earth's core.

Excess hot water carried away to heat homes

Steam turns turbine to produce electricity

Steam emerges

Water pumped underground becomes very hot

GEOTHERMAL POWER
Water pumped underground is turned into high-pressure steam by geothermal heat. The steam returns to the surface under pressure and turns turbines.

Tide water

Barrier

Turbines in barrier turn to produce electricity

TIDAL POWER STATION
Seawater is held back by a barrage as it rises and falls. When there is a difference in height between the water on either side of the barrage, the water escapes through tunnels, turning turbines.

SOLAR ENERGY
The energy of sunlight produces electricity in solar cells by causing **electrons** to leave the **atoms** in a semiconductor. Each electron leaves behind a gap, or **hole**. Other electrons move into the hole, leaving holes in their atoms. This process continues all the way around a circuit. The moving chain of electrons is an electric current.

Sunlight

Top layer of semiconductor material

Current collector

Bottom layer of semiconductor material

Wire to electric circuit

Electrons flow around the circuit

Silicon atom

Top layer has positive charge

Sunlight

Bottom layer has negative charge

Electron is attracted by positive charge

Electron displaced from atom

Electron moves into hole created by displaced electron

MICROSCOPIC VIEW

Solar cells are usually made of silicon crystals

SOLAR CELL

Electromagnetic radiation

ELECTRICITY AND MAGNETISM ARE DIRECTLY related (see pp. 34–37): a changing **electric field** will produce a changing **magnetic field**, and vice versa. Whenever an electric charge, such as that carried by an **electron**, accelerates, it gives out energy in the form of electromagnetic radiation. For example, electrons moving up and down a radio antenna produce a type of radiation known as radio waves. Electromagnetic radiation consists of oscillating electric and magnetic fields. There is a wide range of different types of electromagnetic radiation, called the electromagnetic spectrum, extending from low-energy radio waves to high-energy, short-**wavelength** gamma rays. This includes visible light and X-rays. Electromagnetic radiation can be seen as both a wave motion (see pp. 20–21) and as a stream of particles called **photons** (see pp. 48–49). Both interpretations are useful, since they provide a means for predicting the behavior of electromagnetic radiation.

RADIATION AS PARTICLES AND WAVES

OSCILLATING FIELDS
All electromagnetic radiation has behavior typical of waves, such as **diffraction** and **interference**. It can be thought of as a combination of changing electric and magnetic fields.

Oscillating electric field

Direction of wave's motion is at right angles to the electric and magnetic field

Two fields at right angles

Wavelength

Oscillating magnetic field

PHOTONS
All electromagnetic radiation also has behavior typical of particles. For example, its energy comes in individual bundles called photons.

Photon as wave packet of energy

Red light has long wavelength

PHOTON OF RED LIGHT

Blue photon has about twice the energy of red photon; the shorter the wavelength, the higher the energy

Blue light has shorter wavelength: waves are more tightly packed

PHOTON OF BLUE LIGHT

RADIO WAVES

PRODUCTION OF RADIO WAVES
The electric current in a radio antenna changes direction rapidly, and produces a changing magnetic field around the antenna. This magnetic field produces an electric field, which in turn produces a magnetic field, and so on.

Antenna

Radiation spreads in all directions

Magnetic field

Magnetic field produced by electric current

One section of the radiation

Electric field

Electric circuit called an oscillator produces electric current which changes direction

Changing magnetic field

Electric field produced by changing magnetic field

Direction of wave

One wavelength

Oscillating magnetic field

THE ELECTROMAGNETIC SPECTRUM

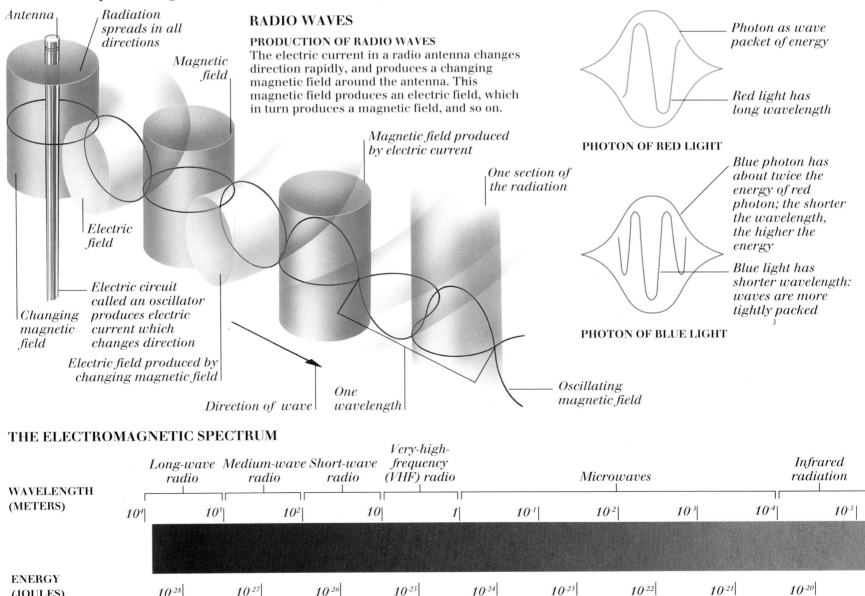

	Long-wave radio	Medium-wave radio	Short-wave radio	Very-high-frequency (VHF) radio	Microwaves	Infrared radiation

WAVELENGTH (METERS)	10^4	10^3	10^2	10	1	10^{-1}	10^{-2}	10^{-3}	10^{-4}	10^{-5}

ENERGY (JOULES)	10^{-28}	10^{-27}	10^{-26}	10^{-25}	10^{-24}	10^{-23}	10^{-22}	10^{-21}	10^{-20}	10

THE WHITE LIGHT SPECTRUM

Human eyes can detect a range of wavelengths of electromagnetic radiation, from "red light" to "blue light." When all of the wavelengths within that range are perceived together, they produce the sensation of white light.

Glass prism

Red light (wavelength: $6.2–7.7 \times 10^{-7}m$)

Orange light (wavelength: $5.9–6.2 \times 10^{-7}m$)

Yellow light (wavelength: $5.7–5.9 \times 10^{-7}m$)

Green light (wavelength: $4.9–5.7 \times 10^{-7}m$)

Blue light (wavelength: $4.5–4.9 \times 10^{-7}m$)

Violet light (wavelength: $3.9–4.5 \times 10^{-7}m$)

X-RAYS

PRODUCTION OF X-RAYS

Near the high-energy end of the electromagnetic spectrum come X-rays. In an X-ray tube, electrons are accelerated by a strong electric field. They then hit a metal target, and their kinetic energy is turned into electromagnetic radiation.

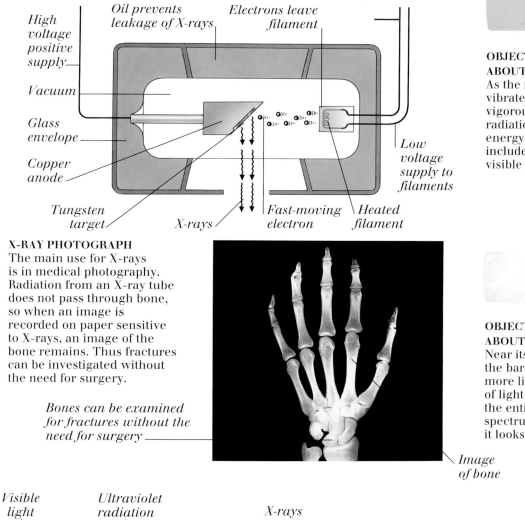

High voltage positive supply

Oil prevents leakage of X-rays

Electrons leave filament

Vacuum

Glass envelope

Copper anode

Tungsten target

X-rays

Fast-moving electron

Heated filament

Low voltage supply to filaments

X-RAY PHOTOGRAPH

The main use for X-rays is in medical photography. Radiation from an X-ray tube does not pass through bone, so when an image is recorded on paper sensitive to X-rays, an image of the bone remains. Thus fractures can be investigated without the need for surgery.

Bones can be examined for fractures without the need for surgery

Image of bone

RADIATION FROM HOT OBJECTS

The **atoms** of a solid vibrate (see pp. 22–23). Atoms contain electric charges in the form of **protons** and electrons. Because they vibrate, these charges produce a range of electromagnetic radiation. The rate of vibration, and therefore the wavelengths of radiation produced, depends on **temperature**, as this steel bar shows.

Hot metal atoms produce some red light   *Steel bar*

OBJECT HEATED TO ABOUT 900K (627°C)
At 900K, objects give out a range of radiation, mainly infrared. The graph shows how much of each wavelength is radiated.

Cooler atoms radiate invisible infrared

No blue light produced

Radiation now appears yellow

OBJECT HEATED TO ABOUT 1,500K (1,227°C)
As the metal atoms vibrate more vigorously, the radiation has more energy. It therefore includes more of the visible spectrum.

More of the spectrum is radiated

Radiation now appears white

OBJECT HEATED TO ABOUT 1,800K (1,527°C)
Near its melting point, the bar produces even more light. The range of light now includes the entire visible spectrum. This is why it looks bright white.

The complete visible spectrum is radiated

Visible light   *Ultraviolet radiation*   *X-rays*   *Gamma rays*

10^{-6} | 10^{-7} | 10^{-8} | 10^{-9} | 10^{-10} | 10^{-11} | 10^{-12} | 10^{-13} | 10^{-14} | 10^{-15} | 10^{-16} | 10^{-17} |

10^{-18} | 10^{-17} | 10^{-16} | 10^{-15} | 10^{-14} | 10^{-13} | 10^{-12} | 10^{-11} | 10^{-10} | 10^{-9} | 10^{-8} |

Color

THE HUMAN EYE CAN ONLY PERCEIVE a small section of the **electromagnetic spectrum** (see pp. 38–39). We call this section "visible light." Different colors across the spectrum of visible light correspond to different **wavelengths** of light. Our eyes contain cells called **cones**, which are sensitive to these different wavelengths and allow us to see in color. Three different types of cone are affected by light in the red, green, and blue parts of the spectrum. These correspond to the **primary colors**. Different light sources give out different parts of the spectrum, which appear as different colors. When combined, colored lights appear as different colors. This is called the **additive process**. Adding primary light sources in the correct proportions can produce the sensation of other colors in our eyes. When light hits a **pigment** in an object, only some colors are reflected. Which colors are **reflected** and which **absorbed** depends on the pigment. This is the **subtractive process**. Looking at a colored object in colored light may make the colors appear different. This is because pigments can only reflect colors that are present in the incoming light.

CONE SENSITIVITY

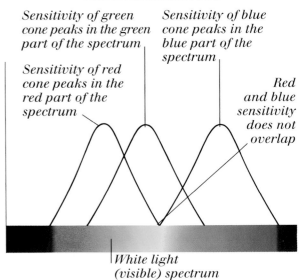

Sensitivity of green cone peaks in the green part of the spectrum

Sensitivity of blue cone peaks in the blue part of the spectrum

Sensitivity of red cone peaks in the red part of the spectrum

Red and blue sensitivity does not overlap

White light (visible) spectrum

COLOR VISION
There are three different types of cone in the normal human eye, each sensitive to a different part of the spectrum. White light stimulates all three types of cone cells.

SOURCES OF LIGHT

This spectrum shows which colors are produced

All colors of light together combine to produce white

BRIGHT FILAMENT LAMP
With a high **electric current**, the whole spectrum of visible light is produced (see p. 39).

BRIGHT FILAMENT LAMP

Red, yellow, and green light combine to produce orange

Lamp appears orange *No blue light produced*

DIM FILAMENT LAMP
With a smaller current, the **temperature** of the **filament** (see pp. 32–33) is low.

DIM FILAMENT LAMP

Lamp produces certain colors in each part of the spectrum

All three types of cone are stimulated and lamp appears white

FLUORESCENT LAMP
In a **fluorescent** lamp, chemicals called **phosphors** produce colors in many parts of the spectrum.

FLUORESCENT LAMP

LED produces colors in the green part of the spectrum

LED appears green

GREEN LED
An LED (light-emitting diode) is made of a **semiconductor**, and produces certain colors of light.

GREEN LED

Two colors of light very close together in the orange part of the spectrum are produced

Lamp appears orange

SODIUM LAMP
In a sodium lamp, an electric current excites electrons in sodium vapour, giving them extra energy. The electrons give the energy out as light.

SODIUM LAMP

Only certain colors characteristic of neon are produced

Lamp appears orange

NEON TUBE
In a similar way to a sodium lamp, a neon discharge lamp produces a characteristic orange glow.

NEON TUBE

ADDITIVE PROCESS

Adding red, green, and blue light in the correct proportions can create the illusion of any other color. These three colors are called primary colors. A color made from adding any two primary colors alone is called a secondary color.

BLUE LIGHT (PRIMARY)

Primary blue light stimulates the blue cone

MAGENTA (SECONDARY)

Primary red and primary blue combine to appear as magenta

CYAN (SECONDARY)

Primary green and primary blue combine to appear as cyan

WHITE LIGHT

All the primary colors together stimulate all types of cone and appear white

GREEN LIGHT (PRIMARY)

Primary green light stimulates the green cone

RED LIGHT (PRIMARY) *Primary red light stimulates the red cone*

PRIMARY COLORS FOR THE ADDITIVE PROCESS

YELLOW (SECONDARY)

Primary red and primary green combine to appear as yellow

SUBTRACTIVE PROCESS

These three filters contain pigments which absorb some of the colors in the white light passing through them from a light beneath. By mixing primary pigments together, all colors except true white can be produced.

The primary pigment colors are different to the primary light colors

CYAN FILTER (PRIMARY)

A primary cyan filter will absorb all light except blue and green

BLUE (SECONDARY)

Magenta and cyan filters together allow blue light through

GREEN (SECONDARY)

Cyan and yellow filters together only allow green light through

BLACK (NO COLOR)

Where all three filters overlap, they absorb all colors, and appear black

YELLOW FILTER (PRIMARY)

A primary yellow filter will absorb all light except red and green

MAGENTA FILTER (PRIMARY)

A primary magenta filter will absorb all light except red and blue

COMBINING PRIMARY COLORED FILTERS FOR THE SUBTRACTIVE PROCESS

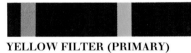

RED (SECONDARY)

Magenta and yellow filters together will allow red light through

COLORED OBJECTS IN COLORED LIGHT

Green pot appears green

White pot reflects all colors

Green pot appears black

Blue pot appears black

Red pot appears black

Blue pot appears black

White pot reflects the blue light and appears blue

Red pot appears red

Green pot appears black

White pot appears green

IN WHITE LIGHT
The green pot only reflects the green part of the spectrum, absorbing the other colors.

IN BLUE LIGHT
When only blue light is available, the green pigment can reflect no green light, and appears black.

IN RED LIGHT
When only red light is available, the green pigment can reflect no green light, and appears black.

IN GREEN LIGHT
When only green light is available, the green pigment reflects green light and appears green.

Reflection and refraction

LIGHT IS A FORM OF **electromagnetic radiation** (see pp. 48–49). In free space, it travels in a straight line at 300 million meters per second. When a beam of light meets an object, a proportion of the rays may be reflected. Some light may also be absorbed, and some transmitted. Without reflection, we would only be able to see objects that give out their own light. Light always reflects from a surface at the same angle at which it strikes it. Thus parallel rays of light meeting a very flat surface will remain parallel when reflected. A beam of light reflecting from an irregular surface will scatter in all directions. Light that passes through an object will be **refracted**, or bent. The angle of refraction depends on the angle at which the light meets the object, and the material from which the object is made. **Lenses** and mirrors can cause light rays to **diverge** or **converge**. When light rays converge, they can reach a point of focus. For this reason, lenses and mirrors can form images. This is useful in binoculars and other optical instruments (see pp. 44–45).

SEEING BY REFLECTED LIGHT
Light travels out from a source and hits objects such as this plant. The plant reflects some of this light, a proportion of which will enter our eyes.

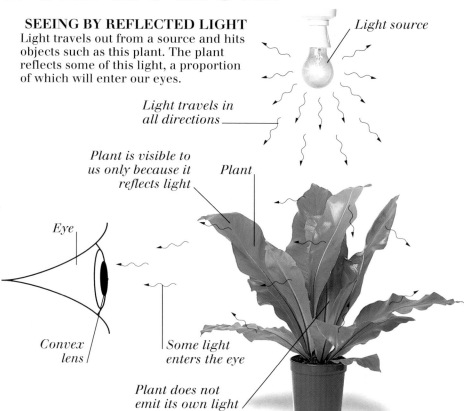

Light source

Light travels in all directions

Plant is visible to us only because it reflects light

Plant

Eye

Convex lens

Some light enters the eye

Plant does not emit its own light

REFLECTING AND REFRACTING
The illustrations below show what happens when parallel beams of light reflect regularly and irregularly and when they refract.

REGULAR REFLECTION

— *Beams remain parallel*

— *Flat surface such as a mirror*

IRREGULAR REFLECTION

— *Beams scatter in all directions*

— *Irregular surface such as paper*

REFRACTION IN A GLASS BLOCK

Light is bent as it enters

Block

Light is bent as it leaves

TOTAL INTERNAL REFLECTION
When light moves from one medium to another, for example from glass to air, some of the light will normally be reflected. When the light striking the boundary reaches a certain angle—the **critical angle**—all of the light reflects back. This is called **total internal reflection**. It is put to use in binoculars, where the light path is folded by prisms so that it can be contained within a compact case.

Light source

Slit produces narrow beam

Small glass prism

DEMONSTRATION OF TOTAL INTERNAL REFLECTION

Light undergoes total internal reflection at glass-air boundary

Eyepiece

Focusing mechanism

Sturdy case

Prism

Light reflects twice in prisms

Total internal reflection

Objective lens

BINOCULARS

LENSES AND MIRRORS

The images below show how beams of light from a bulb are affected by **concave** and **convex** mirrors and lenses. Convex lenses and mirrors have surfaces that curve outward at the center, while concave lenses curve inward and are thicker at the edges.

CONCAVE LENS (BENDS LIGHT OUTWARD)

Light source

Light rays travel out in straight lines

Convex lens bends diverging rays into straight beam

Concave lens

Light rays diverge

CONVEX LENS (BENDS LIGHT INWARD)

Light rays converge

First convex lens produces parallel beam

Convex lens

Focal length

Light focused to a point

CONVEX MIRROR (REFLECTS LIGHT OUTWARD)

Convex mirror

Light source

Convex lens bends diverging rays into a straight beam

Parallel light rays

Light rays diverge as they reflect

CONCAVE MIRROR (REFLECTS LIGHT INWARD)

Concave mirror

Light source

Convex lens bends diverging rays into straight beam

Light rays converge as they reflect

Focal length

LENSES

Concave lenses make objects appear smaller, and allow a larger field of vision. Objects lying within the focal length of a convex lens appear larger.

CONCAVE LENS

Regular squares

A concave lens is often fitted to the rear window of a vehicle to improve a driver's field of vision

Squares appear smaller through lens

Regular squares

CONVEX LENS

A convex lens can be used as a magnifying glass

Squares appear magnified through lens

IMAGE FORMATION

Because they focus light, convex lenses can be used to project images onto a screen. The screen must be placed at a point where the rays focus in order for a clear image to be produced. Only objects that lie within a range of distances from the lens, called the **depth of field**, will be in focus at any one time.

IMAGE INVERTS

Ray 1 starts parallel to optical axis

Ray 3 goes through the focal point in front of the lens

Optical axis

Convex lens

Ray 2 goes through center of lens so is undeviated

Ray 3 is bent parallel to the optical axis

The rays focus on the opposite side of the optical axis so the image is inverted

Ray 1 is bent and goes through focal point of lens

PROJECTED IMAGE

Black arrows drawn on tracing paper

Convex lens

Screen

Focused image on screen

Image is inverted vertically and horizontally

Optical instruments

THE HUMAN EYE CONTAINS A **LENS** that produces an **image** by focusing the light that passes through it. But the eye does not record images, or allow us to see objects that are very small, or very far away. To achieve these tasks, we need to use optical instruments. A camera, for example, records an image on light-sensitive film. To see objects that are very small or very far away, we need to produce a magnified image, which the eye can then observe. By using a compound microscope, light from a very small object can be made to produce a magnified image. A telescope produces a magnified image in a similar way to a microscope, using lenses to focus light. There are limits to the use of optical instruments. Even the most precise lenses suffer from **chromatic aberration** (see opposite)—a problem that can be solved by pairs of lenses known as **achromatic doublets**.

CAMERA

The cutaway view below shows the main features of a single lens reflex (SLR) camera. The light is focused onto film at the back of the camera by a lens or a combination of lenses.

Shutter release button

Light, tight camera body

Pentaprism directs light into viewfinder

45° mirror flipped out of the way to allow light onto film

Film plane

Light reaches film only when this shutter opens

Aperture

Light enters through lens attached to this aperture

COMPOUND MICROSCOPE

Together, the lenses in a microscope produce a magnified image

Eyepiece

Focusing knob

Different objective lens gives different magnification

Objective lens

Three-objective turret

Glass slide

Specimen *Stage*

Angled mirror

Base

MICROSCOPES

A basic optical microscope consists of two lenses, the objective and the eyepiece. Light is focused by the objective, which has a very small **focal length**. The light passes up inside the body tube, and is focused by the eyepiece into the eye.

RED BLOOD CELLS SEEN THROUGH MICROSCOPE

LIGHT PATH THROUGH MICROSCOPE

Eye

Light enters eye

Eyepiece lens focuses light

Light passes through body of microscope

Objective lens focuses light from specimen

Prepared specimen placed on slide

Mirror directs light through the specimen

TELESCOPES

At the front of a **refracting** telescope is an objective lens that collects light and focuses it, producing an image in the telescope's tube. The eyepiece greatly magnifies this image. A **reflecting** telescope uses a mirror instead of an objective lens.

Objective lens

Telescope tube

Small viewfinder telescope used to position larger telescope

Equatorial mount allows user to track stars as they move across the sky

Focusing knob

Prism bends light into eyepiece

Counterbalance

Eyepiece

SMALL REFRACTING TELESCOPE

Tripod

Eyepiece

Concave eyepiece

TELESCOPE IMAGE OF THE MOON
In a telescope, the greater the difference between focal lengths of objective and eyepiece, the greater the magnification. A larger objective lens will yield a brighter image for a given magnification.

REFRACTING TELESCOPE
A **convex** objective lens focuses light from a distant star. The eyepiece is fixed in a tube that can be moved in and out of the telescope tube.

Two rays show the path of light through the telescope

Convex objective lens

Focal point of objective lens

Telescope tube

Light from the object enters through the objective lens

ACHROMATIC DOUBLET
A single lens will refract light of different wavelengths by different amounts. For example, red light focuses at a different point from blue light. This chromatic aberration can be eliminated by using two lenses made of different types of glass.

Red focuses

Rays of white light

Compound lens

All colors focus at the same point

Blue light focuses nearer to lens than red

Single lens

Concave objective mirror

Light from object reflects from objective lens

Eyepiece

REFLECTING TELESCOPE
In this case, a **concave** objective mirror focuses the light. A small plane (flat) mirror directs light through a tube off the side of the telescope to the eyepiece.

Eyepiece lens

Field lens

Flat mirror

Light from objective would focus here

Two rays show the path of light

Telescope tube

Wave behavior

ALL TYPES OF WAVE CAN COMBINE OR INTERFERE. If two waves are in step, so that the peaks coincide, the **interference** results in a wave that will be larger than the original one (**constructive interference**). If the waves are out of step, the peak of one wave will cancel out the trough of another (**destructive interference**). Where the waves are equal in size, they can cancel out entirely. As waves pass around objects or through small openings, they can be **diffracted**, or bent. Diffraction and interference can be observed in water waves, using a ripple tank. The colors seen in soap bubbles are the result of some colors being removed from the white light spectrum by destructive interference. Light reflected off the front and back surfaces of the film interferes. One source of very pure light waves is a laser. The light produced by a laser is coherent. This means that all of the waves are in step and of exactly the same wavelength. The light is produced by a process called stimulated emission. To understand this process, light must be thought of in terms of particles called **photons** (see p.48), as well as waves.

PRINCIPLE OF SUPERPOSITION
When two waves meet, they add up or interfere. This is called the **Principle of Superposition**, and is common to all types of wave.

CONSTRUCTIVE INTERFERENCE
Peak of first wave in step with peak of second

Peak is point of maximum displacement

Peak

When a peak meets a peak, the resulting wave is larger

Trough

DESTRUCTIVE INTERFERENCE
Peak of first wave is in step with trough of second wave

Peak

Trough is the point of minimum displacement

Trough

Where a peak meets a trough, the waves cancel out

DIFFRACTION AND INTERFERENCE

Ring stand

Bright lamp projects light onto table top

Waves diffract around edge

Edge of object placed in water

Electric motor turns eccentric wheel

Wires to power supply

Eccentric wheel moves bar up and down

Support for bar

Oscillating bar or balls creates waves on surface of water

Water

Shallow tank

Rubber tops on legs stop unwanted vibrations

Plane waves created by bar

EDGE DIFFRACTION

Waves radiate in semicircles

Small hole in barrier in water

Plane waves created by bar

DIFFRACTION THROUGH SMALL HOLE

RIPPLE TANK
Diffraction and interference are probably best observed using a ripple tank. A bar moving up and down (oscillating) creates **plane waves** in shallow water. These waves bend around edges and produce semicircular waves after passing through a small hole.

Waves interfere constructively at this point

Waves interfere destructively at this point

Circular wave travels out in all directions

Circular wave produced by oscillating ball

Oscillating ball

INTERFERENCE

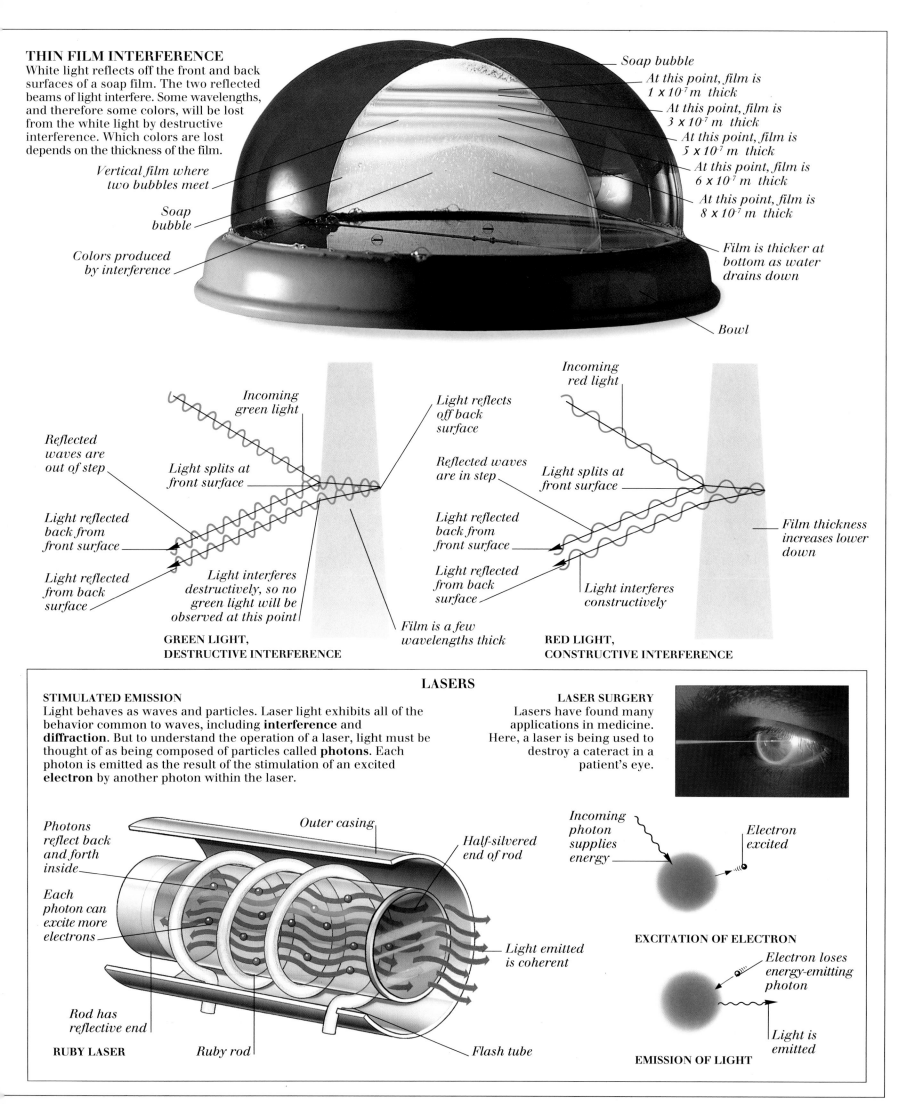

THIN FILM INTERFERENCE
White light reflects off the front and back surfaces of a soap film. The two reflected beams of light interfere. Some wavelengths, and therefore some colors, will be lost from the white light by destructive interference. Which colors are lost depends on the thickness of the film.

Vertical film where two bubbles meet

Soap bubble

Colors produced by interference

Soap bubble

At this point, film is 1×10^{-7} m thick

At this point, film is 3×10^{-7} m thick

At this point, film is 5×10^{-7} m thick

At this point, film is 6×10^{-7} m thick

At this point, film is 8×10^{-7} m thick

Film is thicker at bottom as water drains down

Bowl

Incoming green light

Reflected waves are out of step

Light splits at front surface

Light reflects off back surface

Light reflected back from front surface

Light reflected from back surface

Light interferes destructively, so no green light will be observed at this point

GREEN LIGHT, DESTRUCTIVE INTERFERENCE

Film is a few wavelengths thick

Incoming red light

Light splits at front surface

Reflected waves are in step

Light reflected back from front surface

Light reflected from back surface

Light interferes constructively

Film thickness increases lower down

RED LIGHT, CONSTRUCTIVE INTERFERENCE

LASERS

STIMULATED EMISSION
Light behaves as waves and particles. Laser light exhibits all of the behavior common to waves, including **interference** and **diffraction**. But to understand the operation of a laser, light must be thought of as being composed of particles called **photons**. Each photon is emitted as the result of the stimulation of an excited **electron** by another photon within the laser.

LASER SURGERY
Lasers have found many applications in medicine. Here, a laser is being used to destroy a cateract in a patient's eye.

Photons reflect back and forth inside

Outer casing

Half-silvered end of rod

Each photon can excite more electrons

Light emitted is coherent

Rod has reflective end

RUBY LASER

Ruby rod

Flash tube

Incoming photon supplies energy

Electron excited

EXCITATION OF ELECTRON

Electron loses energy-emitting photon

Light is emitted

EMISSION OF LIGHT

Atoms and electrons

ALL ORDINARY MATTER (see pp. 6–7) consists of tiny particles called atoms. There are 92 naturally occurring types of atom. Each consists of a central, positively charged nucleus (see pp. 50–51), surrounded by negatively charged electrons. An element is a substance made up of one type of atom only. Atoms of different elements have different numbers of electrons. For example, atoms of the element fluorine have nine electrons. Electrons in the atom do not follow definite paths, as planets do, orbiting the Sun. Instead, they are said to be found in regions called orbitals. Electrons in orbitals close to the nucleus have less energy than those farther away and are said to be in the first electron shell. Electrons in the second shell have greater energy. Whenever an excited electron releases its energy by falling to a lower shell, the energy is radiated as light. This is called luminescence. Electrons can be separated from atoms in many ways. In a cathode ray tube, a strong electric field tears electrons away from their atoms. Free electrons in the tube are affected by electric and magnetic fields. Cathode ray tubes are used in television, where a beam of free electrons forms the picture on the screen.

ANATOMY OF A FLUORINE ATOM

A fluorine atom has nine electrons around its nucleus. There are two electrons in the first shell, in an s-orbital (1s). The remaining seven electrons are found in the second shell, two in an s-orbital (2s) and five in p-orbitals (2p).

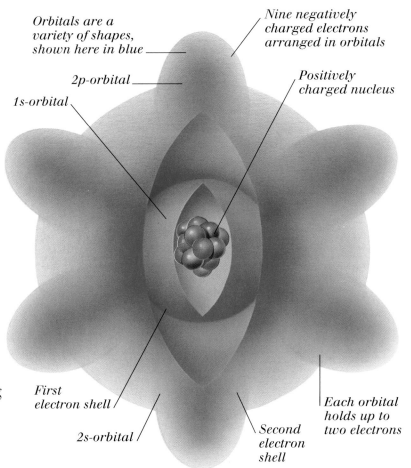

Orbitals are a variety of shapes, shown here in blue

Nine negatively charged electrons arranged in orbitals

2p-orbital

Positively charged nucleus

1s-orbital

First electron shell

2s-orbital

Second electron shell

Each orbital holds up to two electrons

FLUORESCENCE

SOAP POWDER

How does soap powder make clothes appear so bright? Soap powder exhibits a form of luminescence (see above) called **fluorescence**. Electrons around atoms in the powder are excited into high-energy shells by incoming energy, in this case invisible ultraviolet light found in daylight. The electrons fall back to their original shell immediately and reemit the energy as visible light. The color of the light depends upon the difference in energy between the higher and lower shells. This extra light emitted by the powder in the clothes makes them appear bright.

Powder appears white in white light

Soap powder contains substances called optical brighteners

In white light, willemite appears brown

Willemite contains zinc and manganese

Region of quartz

Sodalite is a grayish material in white light

SOAP POWDER IN WHITE LIGHT

WILLEMITE IN WHITE LIGHT

SODALITE IN WHITE LIGHT

Ultraviolet is invisible, so everything normally looks black

Optical brighteners give off blue glow in ultraviolet light

Willemite appears brightly colored in ultraviolet

Electrons absorb ultraviolet and give out yellow light

SOAP POWDER IN ULTRAVIOLET LIGHT

WILLEMITE IN ULTRAVIOLET LIGHT

SODALITE IN ULTRAVIOLET LIGHT

CATHODE RAY TUBE
Inside a cathode ray tube, an **electric current** heats a small filament. The heat generated gives electrons extra energy, moving them farther from their nuclei. A strong electric field then completely removes electrons from their atoms. The free electrons are attracted to the positive **anode**, and pass through it as a cathode ray.

ELECTRON BEAMS

Vacuum

Phosphorescent screen

Maltese cross

Anode connected to positive supply

Wires connecting heater and cathode to power supply

Wire connecting Maltese cross to positive electrical supply

Wire connecting anode to power supply

Beam of electrons (cathode ray) made visible by phosphorescent screen

Glass tube

Support fork

Base

SIDE VIEW

Electron shadow of Maltese cross

Green glow where electrons hit screen

Phosphorescent material

Glass tube

FRONT VIEW

DEFLECTING THE ELECTRONS
Because electrons have electric charge, forces can be applied to them by electric and magnetic fields in the cathode ray tube. The direction of the force depends upon the direction and type of the field.

Screen glows when hit by electrons

Anode connected to positive supply

Glass tube

Vacuum

Electrons travel in straight line

Base

Wire connecting anode to power supply

STRAIGHT CATHODE RAY IN TUBE

Electrons curve in parabolic path due to electric field

Positive terminal

Wires connecting heater and cathode to power supply

Negative terminal

DOWNWARD DEFLECTION BY ELECTRIC FIELD

Electrons travel in part of a circular path due to magnetic field

Helmholtz coil produces magnetic field

4.5V battery

DOWNWARD DEFLECTION BY MAGNETIC FIELD

HOW A TELEVISION WORKS

DEFLECTED ELECTRON BEAMS
At the heart of most televisions is a cathode ray tube. Electron beams are produced at the back of the tube. Coils of wire around the tube create magnetic fields, which deflect the electron beams to different parts of the screen. The screen itself is coated with phosphorescent materials called **phosphors**.

Red, green, and blue electron guns

PHOSPHORESCENCE
When the cathode rays hit the special coating on a television screen, the screen glows because it is phosphorescent. **Phosphorescence** is a form of luminescence where the incoming energy is not reemitted immediately but is stored and reemitted over a period of time. This means that as the cathode ray quickly scans the picture, the phosphor glows for long enough for a whole picture to form.

Electron beams (cathode rays)

Phosphorescent screen

Picture built up as beams scan across the screen

Cathode ray tube

Electromagnetic coils are fed with varying electric signal from antenna which builds up a picture from the electron beam

Electronic circuits process and amplify the signal

Signal received from television antenna consists of a varying electric current

Nuclear physics

AT THE CENTER OF EVERY **ATOM** LIES a positively charged
nucleus. It consists of **protons** and **neutrons**. The number of
protons in the nucleus is called the **atomic number**. Because they
all have the same **electric charge**, protons repel each other.
The nucleus holds together despite this repulsion because of the
strong nuclear force (see pp. 52–53). The balance between the
repulsive force and the strong nuclear force determines whether
a nucleus is stable or unstable. On the whole, small nuclei are
more stable than larger ones, because the strong nuclear force
works best over small distances. An unstable, larger nucleus can
break up or decay in two main ways, **alpha decay** and **beta decay**.
These produce **alpha** and **beta particles**. In each type of decay, the
atomic number of the new nucleus is different from the original
nucleus, because the number of protons present alters. Nuclei can
also completely split into two smaller fragments, in a process
called **fission**. In another **nuclear reaction** called **fusion**, small
nuclei join together. Both of these reactions can release huge
amounts of energy. Fusion provides most of the Sun's energy,
while fission can be used in power stations to produce electricity.

FLUORINE-19 NUCLEUS

The number of protons in a nucleus defines what
element the atom is. For example, all fluorine atoms
have nine protons. Fluorine has an atomic number of 9.
The number of neutrons can vary. Fluorine-19 has ten
neutrons, while fluorine-18 has nine.

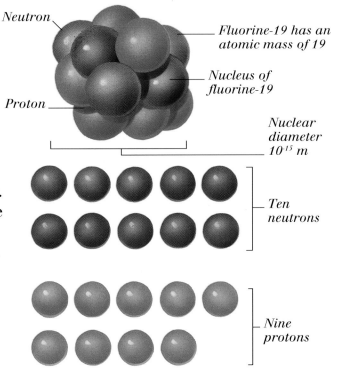

Neutron

*Fluorine-19 has an
atomic mass of 19*

*Nucleus of
fluorine-19*

Proton

*Nuclear
diameter
10^{15} m*

*Ten
neutrons*

*Nine
protons*

RADIOACTIVITY

*Smaller and
potentially
more stable
nucleus*

*Large unstable
nucleus*

*Alpha particle:
two neutrons
and two protons*

*A gamma ray is
also released*

ALPHA DECAY
An unstable nucleus may reduce its
size by releasing an alpha particle.

*Potentially more
stable nucleus*

*Unstable
nucleus*

*New nucleus has one
more proton and one
less neutron*

*Fast electron
(beta particle)*

*A gamma
ray is also
released*

BETA DECAY
In beta decay, a neutron of an unstable nucleus
changes into a proton and an electron. The proton
remains in the nucleus, while the electron is released
at high speed.

ANALYZING RADIOACTIVITY
Because of their electric charges, a strong magnetic field will
deflect alpha and beta rays in a cloud chamber. Cloud chambers
are used to show these paths as in the illustration below.

*Cloud chamber contains
carbon dioxide*

Beta ray

*Drops form, indicating
course of particles, from
which mass and charge
can be calculated*

Alpha ray

*Gamma ray
unaffected by
magnetic field*

Radioactive source

GEIGER-MULLER TUBE
As they pass through the air, alpha and
beta rays hit atoms, separating electrons
and creating **ions**, which can
be detected inside a
Geiger-Müller tube.

*Wire to
detector*

*Radioactive
particles
enter here*

Tube

Base

COSMIC RAYS
The Earth is constantly
bombarded by particles from
space. Most of these are
protons, from atoms of the
most abundant element,
hydrogen. Occasionally, the
protons collide with atoms in
the air, producing showers of
secondary particles called
cosmic rays.

*Tracks left by cosmic rays
in a bubble chamber*

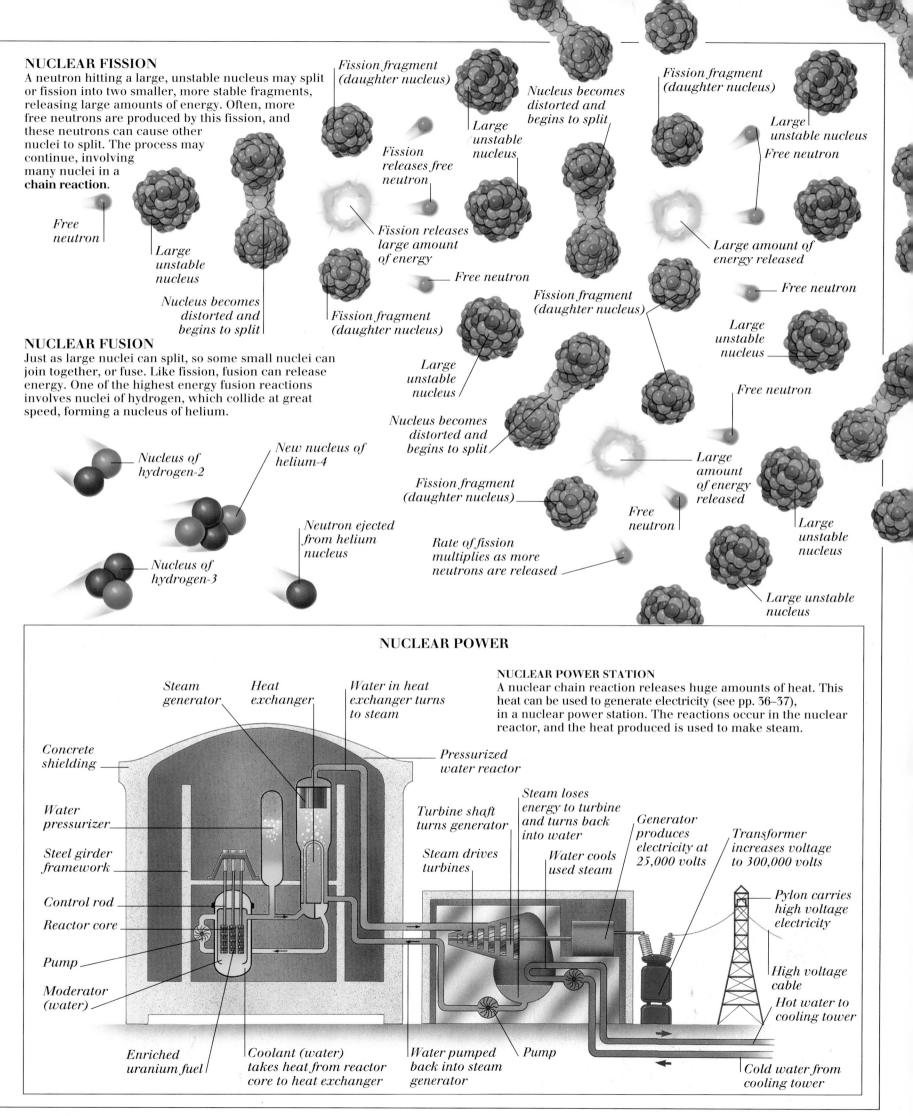

NUCLEAR FISSION
A neutron hitting a large, unstable nucleus may split or fission into two smaller, more stable fragments, releasing large amounts of energy. Often, more free neutrons are produced by this fission, and these neutrons can cause other nuclei to split. The process may continue, involving many nuclei in a **chain reaction.**

Free neutron

Large unstable nucleus

Nucleus becomes distorted and begins to split

Fission fragment (daughter nucleus)

Fission releases free neutron

Fission releases large amount of energy

Free neutron

Fission fragment (daughter nucleus)

Large unstable nucleus

Nucleus becomes distorted and begins to split

Nucleus becomes distorted and begins to split

Fission fragment (daughter nucleus)

Fission fragment (daughter nucleus)

Large unstable nucleus

Free neutron

Large amount of energy released

Free neutron

Large unstable nucleus

Free neutron

Large amount of energy released

Free neutron

Large unstable nucleus

Rate of fission multiplies as more neutrons are released

Large unstable nucleus

NUCLEAR FUSION
Just as large nuclei can split, so some small nuclei can join together, or fuse. Like fission, fusion can release energy. One of the highest energy fusion reactions involves nuclei of hydrogen, which collide at great speed, forming a nucleus of helium.

Nucleus of hydrogen-2

New nucleus of helium-4

Neutron ejected from helium nucleus

Nucleus of hydrogen-3

NUCLEAR POWER

Steam generator

Heat exchanger

Water in heat exchanger turns to steam

NUCLEAR POWER STATION
A nuclear chain reaction releases huge amounts of heat. This heat can be used to generate electricity (see pp. 36–37), in a nuclear power station. The reactions occur in the nuclear reactor, and the heat produced is used to make steam.

Concrete shielding

Pressurized water reactor

Water pressurizer

Turbine shaft turns generator

Steam loses energy to turbine and turns back into water

Generator produces electricity at 25,000 volts

Transformer increases voltage to 300,000 volts

Steel girder framework

Steam drives turbines

Water cools used steam

Control rod

Pylon carries high voltage electricity

Reactor core

Pump

High voltage cable

Moderator (water)

Hot water to cooling tower

Enriched uranium fuel

Coolant (water) takes heat from reactor core to heat exchanger

Water pumped back into steam generator

Pump

Cold water from cooling tower

Particle physics

PARTICLE PHYSICS ATTEMPTS TO EXPLAIN matter and **force** in terms of tiny particles. The **atom**, once thought to be the smallest particle, is actually made of **protons, neutrons,** and **electrons.** But the proton and the neutron are themselves made up of smaller particles, known as **quarks.** There are four types of force acting between matter, namely **gravitational force**, the **electromagnetic force**, the **strong nuclear force,** and the **weak interaction.** According to current theory, each of these forces is explained by the exchange of particles called **gauge bosons** between the particles of matter. For example, the **nucleus** holds together as a result of the exchange of particles called **mesons** (a type of gauge boson) between the protons and neutrons present. These exchanges can be visualized in Feynmann diagrams, which show the particles involved in each type of force. The most important tools of particle physics are particle accelerators, which create and destroy particles in high energy collisions. Analysis of these particles helps to prove or disprove the latest theories about the structure of matter and the origin of forces. One of the current aims of large particle accelerators, such as the Large Hadron Collider at **CERN** (opposite), is to prove the existence of a particle called the **Higgs boson.** It may be responsible for giving all matter mass.

HADRONS

A **hadron** is a particle consisting of quarks. There are six types of quark, including the "up" and "down" quarks. Protons, neutrons, and mesons are examples of hadrons. The quarks of hadrons are held together by **gluons.**

One "down" quark, charge: $-\frac{1}{3}$

One "up" quark, charge: $\frac{2}{3}$

Two "down" quarks, charge: $-\frac{1}{3}$

Anti "down" quark, charge: $\frac{1}{3}$

Gluons

Total charge: 1

Gluons

Two "up" quarks, charge: $\frac{2}{3}$

Total charge: 0

Total charge: 1

"Up" quark, charge: $\frac{2}{3}$

Gluons

PROTON   **NEUTRON**   **PI-PLUS MESON**

FEYNMAN DIAGRAMS

These diagrams show which gauge bosons are exchanged to transfer each of the four forces. The horizontal lines represent the guage boson, whereas the diagonal lines and circles represent the two interacting particles.

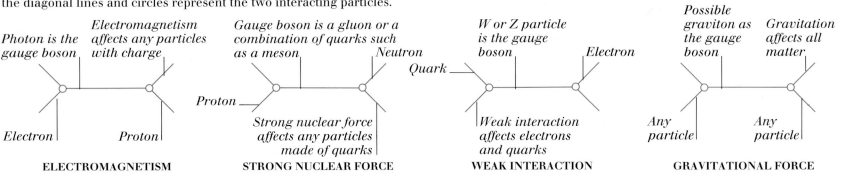

Photon is the gauge boson

Electromagnetism affects any particles with charge

Gauge boson is a gluon or a combination of quarks such as a meson

Neutron

Quark

Proton

W or Z particle is the gauge boson

Electron

Possible graviton as the gauge boson

Gravitation affects all matter

Electron

Proton

Strong nuclear force affects any particles made of quarks

Weak interaction affects electrons and quarks

Any particle

Any particle

ELECTROMAGNETISM   **STRONG NUCLEAR FORCE**   **WEAK INTERACTION**   **GRAVITATIONAL FORCE**

PARTICLE COLLISIONS

The images below show the results of collisions between particles in particle accelerators. Particles of opposite charge curve in different directions in the strong **magnetic field** of the detector.

Spiral tracks of electrons in the bubble chamber

Point of collision

Track of antiproton

Tracks of other particles

ANNIHILATION

When a particle and an antiparticle meet, they destroy each other and become energy. This energy in turn becomes new particles.

Proton

Photon does not leave a track as it has no charge

Tight spiraling electron tracks

A number of particles are created in the collision

PROTON-PHOTON COLLISION

This collision between a **photon** and a proton took place in a type of detector called a bubble chamber. The colors in this photograph have been added for clarity.

Track of a particle called a muon

Incoming electron

Point of collision

Incoming positron

Pi mesons produced by collision

ELECTRON-POSITRON COLLISION

Here, an electron collides with its **antiparticle**, a **positron.** The detector is linked to a computer, which produces this picture of the collision.

THE LARGE HADRON COLLIDER

The Large Hadron Collider (LHC), at CERN near Geneva, will be a huge particle accelerator, in a tunnel about 100 meters below ground. The tunnel will be a ring 27 kilometers long, which is already used for another particle accelerator, the Large Electron Positron (LEP) collider. Two beams of protons will move around in tubes at very high speed, and will be made to collide in detectors, such as the CMS (see below).

Protons and other particles will collide in the detector chambers

Site of detector

Cryogenic unit produces liquid helium

Super proton synchrotron (SPS) ring accelerates protons and injects them into the LHC

Proton synchrotron (PS) ring accelerates protons and injects them into the SPS

Linear injector

Cryogenic unit

Two sets of protons will travel in opposite directions

Site of CMS detector

The ring is 27 km long

Protons in the LHC will travel at close to the speed of light

The ring is between 70 m and 140 m underground

Sauverny
SWISS/FRENCH BORDER
Ségny
Versoix
Ornex
Genthod
Fetney Voltaire
Crozet
Chevry
Sergy
St. Genis-Pouilly
Meyrin
Lake Geneva
GENEVA
Vernier

Pipe containing liquid helium at 4.5K (-268.7°C)

Radiation shield

Thermal shield

Iron yoke prevents the magnetic field from leaking out

Electromagnets are kept extremely cold by liquid helium

Collars hold tubes in place

Tube holding proton beams

Each tube is 0.056 m in diameter

Quench discharge pipe

Pipe containing helium gas that removes heat

Support post

One beam of protons enters here

Different layers of detector detect different particles

Very forward calorimeter

Collision takes place here

Hadron calorimeter

Superconducting coil

Coils of electromagnet

One beam of protons enters here

THE ACCELERATOR
In the main experiment of the LHC, protons injected into the ring will be accelerated to nearly the speed of light, traveling in opposite directions in two tubes. **Centripetal force** provided by powerful **electromagnets** keeps the protons moving in a circle.

THE COMPACT SOLENOIDAL (CMS) DETECTOR
Several detectors will be built for detecting the particles produced by collisions in the LHC. The detectors have different parts that detect different types of particle. The hadron calorimeter, for example, can only detect hadrons.

Formulas

MANY OF THE PRINCIPLES EXPLAINED IN THIS BOOK can be expressed as formulas. The use of symbols to represent different values enables the physicist to make quick calculations, reducing even complicated physical phenomena to simple mathematical formulas.

WEIGHT
Weight is equal to mass multiplied by acceleration due to gravity

$$W = mg$$

W = weight
m = mass
g = acceleration due to gravity

TURNING FORCE
Turning force is equal to force multiplied by distance of applied force from pivot

$$T = Fd$$

T = turning force (moment)
F = applied force
d = distance

PRESSURE
Pressure is equal to force applied divided by area over which force acts

$$P = F/A$$

P = pressure
F = applied force
A = area over which force acts

FORCE AND MOTION

NEWTON'S SECOND LAW
Acceleration is equal to force divided by mass

$$a = F/m$$

SPEED
Speed is equal to distance divided by time

$$v = d/t$$

CONSTANT ACCELERATION
Acceleration is equal to change in speed divided by time taken for that change

$$a = v_2 - v_1/t$$

MOMENTUM
Momentum is equal to mass multiplied by speed

$$p = mv$$

F = applied force
v = speed
t = time
d = distance
p = momentum
m = mass
a = acceleration

GRAVITATION
Gravitational force equals a constant, multiplied by mass one, multiplied by mass two, divided by the distance between the masses squared

$$F = Gm_1m_2/d^2$$

F = gravitational force between two objects
G = gravitational constant
m_1 = mass of object one
m_2 = mass of object two
d = distance between the two objects

FRICTION
Frictional force between two surfaces is equal to the coefficient of friction multiplied by the force acting to keep the surfaces together

$$F = \mu N$$

F = frictional force
μ = coefficient of friction; this varies with materials
N = force between two surfaces

AIR RESISTANCE
Force is proportional to speed

$$F \alpha v$$

F = force of resistance due to air
v = speed of motion through air

WORK
Work is equal to force multiplied by distance

$$W = Fd$$

W = work done
F = applied force
d = distance moved in line with force

CENTRIPETAL FORCE
Force is equal to mass multiplied by the speed squared divided by the radius

$$F = mv^2/r$$

F = centripetal force
m = mass of object
v = speed of circular motion
r = radius of object's path

LIQUID PRESSURE
Pressure is equal to the liquid's density multiplied by acceleration due to gravity multiplied by height of water above point

$$P = \rho gh$$

P = pressure
ρ = liquid density
g = acceleration due to gravity
h = height of water above measured point

ELASTICITY
The extension of a solid is proportional to the force applied to it

$$F \alpha x$$

x = extension of solid
F = applied force

GAS LAWS

BOYLE'S LAW
Volume is proportional to one divided by pressure

$$V \alpha 1/P$$

CHARLES' LAW
Volume is proportional to temperature

$$V \alpha T$$

PRESSURE LAW
Pressure is proportional to temperature

$$P \alpha T$$

THE IDEAL GAS EQUATION
Pressure multiplied by volume is equal to ideal gas constant multiplied by temperature

$$PV = RT$$

V = volume
P = pressure
T = temperature
R = the ideal gas constant

ELECTRIC CIRCUITS

OHM'S LAW
Current is equal to voltage divided by resistance

$$I = V/R$$

POWER
Power is equal to voltage multiplied by current

$$P = VI$$

I = current
V = voltage
R = resistance
P = power

IMAGE FORMATION
One divided by the focal length is equal to one divided by the object's distance from lens added to one divided by distance from the lens to the image

$$1/f = 1/u + 1/v$$

f = focal length
u = object's distance from lens
v = distance from lens to image

Appendix: useful data

PHYSICISTS USE STANDARD UNITS of measurement called SI units (Système International), which include the kilogram, the meter, and the second. In addition to these standard units, there are many other units of measurement. The tables below give details of these.

TEMPERATURE SCALES

To convert	Into	Equation
Celsius (C)	Fahrenheit (F)	$F = (C \times 9 \div 5) + 32$
Fahrenheit	Celsius	$C = (F - 32) \times 5 \div 9$
Celsius	Kelvin (K)	$K = C + 273$
Kelvin	Celsius	$C = K - 273$
Fahrenheit	Kelvin	$K = ((F - 32) \times 5 \div 9) + 273$

METRIC – IMPERIAL CONVERSIONS

To convert	Into	Multiply by
Length		
Centimeters	inches	0.3937
Meters	feet	3.281
Kilometers	miles	0.6214
Meters	yards	1.094
Mass		
Grams	ounces	0.03527
Kilograms	pounds	2.205
Metric tonnes	tons	1.102
Area		
Square centimeters	square inches	0.1550
Square meters	square feet	10.76
Hectares	acres	2.471
Square kilometers	square miles	0.3861
Square meters	square yards	1.196
Volume		
Cubic centimeters	cubic inches	0.06102
Cubic meters	cubic feet	35.31
Capacity		
Liters	pints (liquid)	1.760
Liters	gallons (liquid)	0.2200

IMPERIAL – METRIC CONVERSIONS

To convert	Into	Multiply by
Length		
Inches	centimeters	2.540
Feet	meters	0.3048
Miles	kilometers	1.609
Yards	meters	0.9144
Mass		
Ounces	grams	28.35
Pounds	kilograms	0.4536
Tons	metric tonnes	0.9072
Area		
Square inches	square centimeters	6.452
Square feet	square meters	0.09290
Acres	hectares	0.4047
Square miles	square kilometers	2.590
Square yards	square meters	0.8361
Volume		
Cubic inches	cubic centimeters	16.39
Cubic feet	cubic meters	0.02832
Capacity		
Pints (liquid)	liters	0.5683
Gallons (liquid)	liters	4.546

PHYSICS SYMBOLS

Symbol	Meaning
α	alpha particle
β	beta particle
γ	gamma ray: photon
ϵ	electromotive force
η	efficiency; viscosity
λ	wavelength
μ	micro-; permeability
ν	frequency; neutrino
ρ	density; resistivity
σ	conductivity
c	speed of light

POWERS OF TEN

Factor	Name	Prefix	Symbol
10^{18}	quintillion	exa-	E
10^{15}	quadrillion	peta-	P
10^{12}	trillion	tera-	T
10^{9}	billion	giga-	G
10^{6}	million	mega-	M
10^{3}	thousand	kilo-	k
10^{2}	hundred	hecto-	h
10^{1}	ten	deca-	da
10^{-1}	one tenth	deci-	d
10^{-2}	one hundredth	centi-	c
10^{-3}	one thousandth	milli-	m
10^{-6}	one millionth	micro-	μ
10^{-9}	one billionth	nano-	n
10^{-12}	one trillionth	pico-	p
10^{-15}	one quadrillionth	femto-	f
10^{-18}	one quintillionth	atto-	a

The above terms are those used in the US. In the UK one billion is known as one thousand million and one trillion is known as one billion.

BASE SI UNITS

Physical quantity	SI unit	Symbol
Length	meter	m
Mass	kilogram	kg
Time	second	s
Electric current	ampere	A
Temperature	kelvin	K
Luminous intensity	candela	cd
Amount of substance	mole	mol
Plane angle	radian	rad
Solid angle	steradian	sr

DERIVED SI UNITS

Physical quantity	SI unit	Symbol
Frequency	hertz	Hz
Energy	joule	J
Force	newton	N
Power	watt	W
Pressure	pascal (newtons per square meter)	Pa (Nm^{-2})
Electric charge	coulomb	C
Voltage	volt	V
Electric resistance	ohm	Ω

Glossary

ABSOLUTE ZERO: The lowest possible **temperature**. The higher the temperature of matter, the more movement, or **kinetic energy**, its particles possess. At absolute zero the particles do not move at all. Absolute zero is zero **kelvin**, -273.15° **Celsius** or -459.67° **Fahrenheit**.

ACCELERATION: A change in the **speed** of an object. A reduction in speed is a negative acceleration, and is often called a deceleration. Acceleration is usually measured in ms^{-2} (meters per second per second, or meters per second squared).

ACHROMATIC DOUBLET: A system of two **lenses** that eliminates **chromatic aberration**. The two lenses are made of different types of glass.

ADDITIVE PROCESS: Combining light of different colors. When light of more than one color enters the eye, the result is a color that is different from each of the initial colors. This is due to human eyes having three types of **cone** cell. The brain combines the signals from each type of cone, and interprets the result.

ADHESIVE FORCES: The attractive **forces** between two different types of matter, such as water and glass. The balance between adhesive and **cohesive** forces determines whether the **meniscus** of a liquid will be upward or downward.

CHARLES' LAW

ALPHA DECAY/PARTICLE: The breakup of an unstable atomic **nucleus**, resulting in the release of a particle consisting of two **protons** and two **neutrons**—an alpha particle. During alpha decay, the **atomic number** of the nucleus reduces by two and the **atomic mass** by four (see **beta decay**).

AMORPHOUS SOLID: Any solid with particles not arranged in a regular, repeating pattern and therefore not composed of **crystals**. Because the particles are not regularly arranged, over a period of time, an amorphous solid can flow, and is often called a supercooled liquid.

AMPLITUDE: The intensity of a wave motion. For a sound wave, the amplitude determines how loud the sound will be. For a water wave, the amplitude is the height of the wave, half the distance from the peak to the trough.

ANGULAR MOMENTUM The product of the speed of rotation and the **moment** of **inertia** of a spinning object. The moment of inertia of an object is a measure of how hard it is to set the object spinning.

LUBRICATION

ANODE: The positive electrode of any electrical apparatus. Because the anode is connected to the positive electrical supply, **electrons** are attracted to it. Anodes are used in X-ray tubes and **cathode ray tubes**.

ANTIPARTICLE: A particle that has the same **mass** as another particle, but has one or more of its properties equal and opposite.

ATOM: A tiny particle. The building blocks of matter, atoms are the smallest part of an **element**. Atoms are typically 10^{-10}m (or one ten-millionth of a millimeter) in diameter, and consist of a positively charged **nucleus** surrounded by negatively charged **electrons**.

ATOMIC MASS: The total mass of **protons** and **neutrons** in the **nucleus** of an **atom**, expressed in atomic mass units. Protons and neutrons each have a mass of one atomic mass unit. Fluorine-19, with nine protons and ten neutrons, has an atomic mass of nineteen.

ATOMIC NUMBER: The number of **protons** present in the **nucleus** of an **atom**. All fluorine atoms have an

atomic number of nine, because they have nine protons.

BETA DECAY/PARTICLE: The breakup of an unstable atomic **nucleus**, resulting in the release of a fast-moving **electron**. This electron is called a beta particle. During beta decay, the **atomic number** of the nucleus actually increases by one, because a **neutron** changes into a **proton**, releasing an **electron**. The **atomic mass** is unchanged (see **alpha decay**).

BROWNIAN MOTION: The random motion of small solid objects, such as smoke particles, which can be observed under a microscope. The movement is caused by **atoms** and **molecules** of liquid or gas bombarding the solid objects.

BUBBLE CHAMBER: A device used to detect particles in collisions that take place in particle accelerators. The chamber contains a liquid, such as liquid hydrogen, held just below its boiling point. Any particles that have **electric charge** cause **atoms** in the liquid to become **ions**. The liquid boils around these ions, forming tiny gas bubbles wherever a charged particle passes. A strong **magnetic field** in the chamber causes the particles to travel in curved tracks, and each of the particle types can be identified by their tracks.

CAPILLARY ACTION: The rising or falling of a liquid in a narrow tube, above or below the liquid surface, due to surface tension. If **adhesive forces** are stronger than **cohesive forces**, as in the case of water in glass tubes, the liquid will climb up the tube. The narrower the tube, the higher the liquid will rise or fall.

CATHODE: The negative electrode of any electrical apparatus. Because the cathode is connected to the negative electrical supply, **electrons** are pushed away from it (see **anode**).

CATHODE RAY TUBE: A sealed glass tube used in the display of most televisions. Inside the tube,

GYROSCOPE

electrons leave a **cathode**, and are attracted toward the high-**voltage anode**. The electrons form a beam, sometimes called a cathode ray, which can be observed as it touches a **luminescent** screen.

CELSIUS: A **temperature** scale on which water freezes at 0° and boils at 100°. Each degree celsius is equal to one **kelvin**, but the kelvin scale begins at absolute zero (-273.15°C). Once called the Centigrade scale, the name was changed in 1948.

CENTER OF GRAVITY: The point of an object at which clockwise and counterclockwise **moments** are equal and the object therefore balances.

CENTRIPETAL FORCE: The **force** needed to keep an object moving in a circle or an **ellipse**. In the case of circular motion, the force is always directed to the center of the circle, and depends upon the **mass** and **speed** of the object and the radius of the circle.

CERN (CONSEIL EUROPEEN POUR LA RECHERCHE NUCLEAIRE): The European Laboratory for Nuclear Physics, near Geneva on the Swiss-French border and run by nineteen European nations. It is the site of the Large Hadron Collider.

CHAIN REACTION: A process, such as nuclear fission, in which each reaction is in turn the stimulus of a further reaction.

CHARGE: See **electric charge**.

CHROMATIC ABERRATION: A defect in a **lens**, caused by the fact that different **wavelengths** of light refract by different amounts as they pass through glass. The result of the defect is that different colors of light focus at different points. An image produced by the lens therefore has colored fringes around it, often appearing distorted. The problem can be solved by using an **achromatic doublet**.

FOCUSING AN IMAGE

CLOUD CHAMBER: A device used to detect and track particles resulting from radioactive decay. It is a sealed unit containing a vapor, usually alcohol, just at the point of condensing to form a liquid. **Alpha** and **beta** particles possess **electric charge**, and for this reason provide sites around which the vapor can condense. The tracks of the particles appear as paths of tiny droplets (see **bubble chamber**).

COHESIVE FORCES
The attractive **forces** between atoms or molecules in a liquid, such as water. Cohesive forces are responsible for **surface tension** (see **adhesive forces**).

COMPONENT
The effect of a **force** in a particular direction. A force can be thought of as a combination of two or more components.

COMPRESSION
The action of squashing a substance, so that it takes up a smaller space. When a **gas** is compressed, its **pressure** increases. When a solid is compressed reaction forces are produced. These forces are responsible for the strength of a solid such as concrete, which is said to be "strong in compression."

CONCAVE: Shaped like the inside of a bowl. Concave mirrors make parallel light **converge**. Concave **lenses** make parallel light **diverge**.

CONDUCTIVE: Describes a material that allows **electric current** to flow through it easily. A material with a high conductivity allows electricity to flow easily, and is called a conductor. The term can be used to describe heat flow as well as the flow of electricity.

CONES: Cells on the surface at the back of the human eye (the retina), which are sensitive to light of particular ranges of color. The cones allow for color vision. There are three types of cone cell: red-, green-, and blue-sensitive.

CONSTRUCTIVE INTERFERENCE: The combination of two waves where the waves are "in step." Hence the peaks of one wave correspond to the peaks of the other. The **amplitude** of the resulting combined wave is the sum of the amplitudes of the individual waves.

CONVERGE: To come together, as parallel light does, when it comes to a point of focus.

CONVEX: Shaped like the outside of a bowl. Convex **lenses** make parallel light **converge**. Convex mirrors make parallel light **diverge**.

CRITICAL ANGLE: The angle at or above which light striking the boundary between two different materials undergoes **total internal reflection**.

CRYOGENIC UNIT: A cooling device used to reduce the temperature of substances to very low values, often only a few degrees above **absolute zero** (zero kelvin). Cryogenic units are used in particle accelerators, such as those at **CERN**, to produce liquid helium, which cools **electromagnets** necessary for the operation of the accelerator.

CRYSTAL LATTICE: A regular, repeating arrangement of **atoms** or **molecules** in a solid (see **unit cell**).

CRYSTALS: Solids whose atoms or molecules are arranged in a **crystal lattice**.

CURRENT: See **electric current**.

DENSITY: A measure of the concentration of **mass** in a substance. The numerical value for density is calculated by dividing the mass of a given amount of the substance by its **volume**.

DESTRUCTIVE INTERFERENCE: The combination of two waves where the waves are "out of step." This means that the peaks of one wave correspond to the troughs of the other wave. The **amplitude** of the combined wave is therefore reduced.

DIFFRACTION: The bending of waves around the edge of an object. A small gap consists of two edges, so the waves are bent into concentric curves.

DIFFUSION: The mixing of substances, caused by the random motion of their particles. Diffusion is most noticeable in **gases**, because the movement of the particles is much faster than it is in solids or liquids.

DISPLACEMENT: A movement away or the distance of an object from its normal position.

DIVERGE: To move apart, as parallel light does when it passes through a concave **lens**.

DOMAINS: Tiny regions, between 0.1 and 1 mm in width, within magnetic materials. Every **atom** of a magnetic substance, such as iron, is itself a tiny magnet. All of the atoms within a given domain are lined up, so that each domain is magnetized in a particular direction. In an unmagnetized state, the domains cancel each other out. When a material is magnetized, all of the domains are made to line up with each other.

LIGHT-EMITTING DIODE

ELASTICITY: The ability of a substance to regain its size and shape after being stretched by **forces** of **tension**. Forces of attraction between **atoms** within the substance are made stronger when the atoms are pulled apart. These forces are responsible for elasticity.

ELECTRIC CHARGE: A property of certain particles or substances that results in **electrostatic forces**. There are two types or signs of charge: positive and negative. The numbers of positive and negative charges in matter is normally balanced, giving no overall charge (see **ion**).

ELECTRIC CURRENT: The movement of particles with **electric charge**. Most electric currents are the result of moving **electrons**. The movement of electrons is caused by **electrostatic** or **electromagnetic forces**.

ELECTRIC FIELD: A region in which a particle with **electric charge** will experience an **electrostatic force**.

ELECTRODE: Part of an electrical device that is connected to the electrical supply. The positive electrode is called the **anode**, while the negative electrode is called the **cathode**.

ELECTROMAGNET: A device made by winding a continuous coil of wire around an iron core. **Electric current** flowing through the wire creates magnetism that lines up the **domains** in the iron, turning it into a temporary magnet.

ELECTROMAGNETIC FORCES: The **forces** on **electric charges** moving in a **magnetic field**. The size and direction of the force depends upon the speed, sign, and size of the charge, and on the strength and direction of the magnetic field.

ELECTROMAGNETIC RADIATION: A form of energy that travels through space and matter. It is associated with **electric fields** and **magnetic fields**, and can be thought of as a wave motion involving these fields. It can also be thought of as a stream of particles called **photons**. The many types of radiation include light, radio waves, and X-rays.

ELECTROMAGNETIC SPECTRUM: The range of different types of **electromagnetic radiation**. Each type of radiation is identical except for its **wavelength** and its energy. Radiation with short wavelengths and high energy include X-rays and gamma rays, while longer-wavelength, lower-energy radiation includes infrared and radio waves.

ELECTRON: A particle found in all **atoms**. All electrons have one unit of negative **electric charge**.

ELECTROSCOPE: An instrument for measuring the extent of imbalanced **electric charge** in an object. The most common example consists of a glass box with two pieces of gold foil that are pushed apart as they are charged by **induction**.

ELECTROSTATIC FORCES: The forces between electric charges. Two charges of the same sign will push apart, or repel. Charges of different sign pull together, or attract.

ELEMENT: A substance consisting of only one type of **atom**. Examples are hydrogen, oxygen, and fluorine.

ELLIPSE: A shape that looks like a flattened circle. The orbits of the planets are ellipses.

EQUILIBRIUM: A balanced state at which the **resultant** of a number of **forces** on an object is zero.

SOAP BUBBLE

INDUCTION

ERROR BAR: A vertical or horizontal line that is drawn on a **graph** to indicate the margin of accuracy with which a particular measurement was taken.

EVAPORATION: The loss of **atoms** or **molecules** from a liquid, as they break free of the liquid to become a vapor. Evaporation takes place below the boiling temperature of the liquid.

EXCITED: In possession of extra energy. **Electrons** in **atoms** can be excited by heat or light energy. When they do so, they occupy a new position in the atom, according to their new energy.

FAHRENHEIT: Scale of **temperature** on which water freezes at 32 degrees and boils at 212 degrees.

FILAMENT: The fine wire in an incandescent light bulb. The filament heats up when electric current flows through it. At high temperatures, the filament glows.

FISSION: The splitting of unstable **nuclei** of **atoms**. The process begins as a free **neutron** joins the nucleus, making it more unstable. The nucleus splits into two smaller, more stable nuclei and releases further free neutrons and a large amount of energy in a **chain reaction**. This release of energy is used in atom bombs

FLUID: Any substance that flows. Liquids and gases are both fluids.

FLUORESCENCE: A type of **luminescence** in which a substance glows with visible light immediately after being **excited** by invisible ultraviolet radiation.

FOCAL LENGTH: The distance from a **lens** or curved mirror at which a parallel beam of light comes to a focus.

FORCE: A push or a pull.

FREQUENCY: The regularity with which something happens. It is most often applied to a wave or vibration. The number of times the complete cycle of a wave happens each second is the frequency of the wave, and is measured in hertz (Hz).

FULCRUM: The point about which an object turns. For example, the fulcrum of a lever is its pivot.

FUSION: A joining of small **nuclei** of **atoms** to form larger nuclei. In some cases, such as when hydrogen atoms fuse to form atoms of the **element** helium, there is a huge release of energy during the process.

GAUGE BOSON: A particle exchanged between two interacting particles. At the sub-microscopic level of the tiniest particles, the exchange is responsible for the four forces: **gravity, electromagnetic force**, the **weak interaction**, and the **strong nuclear force**.

GEIGER–MULLER TUBE: A device for detecting radioactivity. An **electric current** flows between the wall of the tube and a metal wire at its center when **alpha** or **beta particles** enter.

GENERATOR: A machine that produces an electrical **voltage** whenever its rotor is turned. The **kinetic energy** of the rotor becomes electrical energy because of the coils and magnets.

GLUONS: Particles responsible for carrying the **strong nuclear force** (see **gauge boson**), according to modern theory.

GRAPH: A visual representation of an experiment's results. A graph will highlight any relationships between the various types of data.

GRAVITY/GRAVITATION: A force of attraction between all objects with **mass**. The size of the force depends upon the masses of the two objects and the distance between the objects. Modern theory says that gravity is carried by particles known as gravitons (see **gauge boson**).

GYROSCOPE
Usually thought of as a spinning metal disk supported in a metal cage, the word can refer to any spinning object. Gyroscopes have stability as they spin.

HADRON
Any particle that is composed of **quarks**. Examples are the **proton** and the pi **meson**.

HIGGS BOSON: Hypothetical particle whose existence would link the **electromagnetic force** and the **weak interaction**, and explain why particles have **mass**.

HOLE: A vacant electron position within the **crystal lattice** of a **semiconductor** that can be thought of as a positive charge.

IMAGE: A picture formed by a lens or a curved mirror. Images cast on screens by convex lenses are called real images, while those seen using telescopes or microscopes, which cannot be directly projected, are called virtual images.

INDUCTION: 1. The apparent charging of one object by an electrically charged object nearby. The charging is apparent since it is only a shift of **electric charge** within the object. 2. The magnetization of iron objects in the presence of a magnet. The **domains** inside the iron line up with the **magnetic field** of the magnet.

INERTIA: The resistance of an object to any change in its motion.

INFRARED RADIATION: A type of **electromagnetic radiation**, with a **wavelength** shorter than visible light.

INTERFERENCE: The combination of two or more waves.

MENISCUS

ION: An **atom** with an overall electric charge. The numbers of positively charged protons and of negatively charged electrons in an atom are normally equal. But the removal of one or more electrons leaves the atom with a net positive charge, while extra electrons give a net negative charge.

KELVIN: The absolute scale of **temperature**, the Kelvin scale begins at absolute zero, and unlike the **Celsius** and **Fahrenheit** scales, does not rely on fixed points.

KINETIC ENERGY: The energy of a moving object, dependent upon the mass and speed of the object.

LATENT HEAT: Heat energy that melts a solid or vaporizes a liquid. Latent heat does not raise the temperature of the substance.

LENS: A curved piece of glass or other transparent material that refracts light, and can form **images**.

LIMITING FRICTION: The **force** which must be overcome to start an object moving when it is in contact with a surface. It is greatest between rough surfaces.

LUMINESCENCE: The emission of light due to a decrease in the energy level of an **excited electron** within an **atom** or **molecule**. The two main types are **fluorescence** and **phosphorescence**.

MAGNETIC FIELD: A field of **force** around the poles of a magnet or a wire carrying an **electric current**.

MASS: The measure of an object's **inertia**. Mass is also defined by **gravitation**. The gravitational force between two objects depends upon their masses.

MELTING POINT: The temperature at which a solid substance becomes a liquid. It is dependent upon atmospheric **pressure**.

MENISCUS: The curved surface of a liquid where it meets the container. It is caused by a combination of **adhesive** and **cohesive forces**.

MESONS: A **hadron** consisting of two quarks. An example is the pi meson, which carries the **strong nuclear force** between **protons** and **neutrons** within the **nucleus**.

MICROMETER: A device used to measure very small displacements.

MOLECULE: The smallest amount of a compound. A water molecule consists of two **atoms** of hydrogen and one of oxygen.

MOMENT: The turning effect of a **force**.

NEUTRON: One of the particles in the **nucleus** of an **atom**. It is a **hadron**, and has no **electric charge**.

NEWTON METER: A device used to measure **force**. A pointer moves along a scale as a spring inside the meter extends. The extension of the spring depends upon the applied force.

NUCLEAR REACTIONS: Changes involving the **nuclei** of **atoms**, such as **fission** and **fusion**.

NUCLEUS: The central part of an **atom**. It has a positive **electric charge** because it contains **protons**.

ORBITALS: Regions of an **atom** in which **electrons** are found. The name comes from the word "orbit," since electrons were

MAGNETIC FIELD

originally thought to follow definite paths around the **nucleus**.

OSCILLATOR: An electric circuit that produces an alternating **electric current**, which repeatedly changes direction.

PERMANENT MAGNETS: Objects with a fixed magnetism. The **domains** in a permanent magnet always align to produce a **magnetic field** (see **electromagnet**).

PHOSPHORESCENCE (PHOSPHOR): A type of **luminescence** in which a substance glows with visible light some time after being **excited** (see **fluorescence**). A phosphor is any substance exhibiting phosphorescence.

PHOTON: A particle of **electromagnetic radiation**. The **energy** of a photon depends only upon the **wavelength** of the radiation. A photon can be thought of as a packet of waves.

PLANE WAVE: A wave motion in which the waves are parallel to one another and perpendicular to the direction of the wave's motion.

POSITRON: The **antiparticle** of the **electron**. It is identical to the electron in every way, except that it has positive **electric charge**.

POTENTIAL ENERGY: Energy that is "stored." An object held in the air has potential energy by virtue of its height and the **gravitational force** pulling it downward.

PRESSURE: A measure of the concentration of a **force**. The pressure exerted by a force is equal to the size of the force divided by the area over which it acts. Solids, liquids and gases exert pressure.

PRIMARY COLORS: A set of three colors, which, when combined in the correct proportion, can produce any other color. The set of

ONE KG MASS

primaries for the **additive process** is different from that for the **subtractive process**.

PRINCIPLE OF SUPERPOSITION: The rules governing the **interference** of waves.

PRINCIPLE OF THE CONSERVATION OF ENERGY: Energy can be neither created nor destroyed, it can only change, or transfer, from one form to another.

PROTON: A **hadron** found within the **nucleus** of an **atom**. It has a positive **electric charge**.

QUARKS: Particles that combine together to form **hadrons**, such as **protons** and **neutrons**. No quark has ever been detected in isolation.

RAREFACTION: The lowering of the **density** and **pressure** of a gas; the opposite of **compression**.

REACTION: A **force** produced by an object that is equal and opposite to a force applied to the object.

REFRACTION: The bending of light or other **electromagnetic radiation** as it passes from one material to another.

RESISTANCE: A measure of the opposition to the flow of **electric current**. It is the ratio of **voltage** to current.

RESULTANT: The combined effect of two or more **forces**.

SANKEY DIAGRAM: An illustration of the energy changes in a process. The diagram consists of a large arrow, which represents the input of energy to the process, and which splits according to the energy changes that occur.

SEMICONDUCTOR: A material in which the **electrons** are held only loosely to their **atoms**. The electrons can become free, and the material therefore becomes **conductive**, with only a small input of **energy**.

SHELL: An energy level occupied by **electrons** within an **atom**. It is generally true that the lower the energy of electrons in the shell, the closer it is to the **nucleus**.

SI UNITS (SYSTEME INTERNATIONAL D'UNITES): A system of units accepted by the worldwide scientific community as the standard. Its seven base units include the kilogram and second.

SOLENOID: A long coil of wire, which produces a **magnetic field**

similar to that of a bar magnet. With an iron bar inside the coil, a solenoid becomes an **electromagnet**.

SOLUTION: A liquid mixture of substances in which the particles of the substances are uniformly mixed.

SPEED: The rate at which an object moves, equal to the distance moved divided by the time taken.

STATE: The form of a substance, either solid, liquid, or gas.

STRONG NUCLEAR FORCE: The **force** between **hadrons**. It is carried by **gluons**, or by combinations of **quarks** (see **gauge boson**). The strong nuclear force is responsible for holding the **nucleus** together.

SUBTRACTIVE PROCESS: The process by which pigments absorb parts of the visible spectrum of light, but reflect others, making objects appear to have color.

SUPERCOOLED LIQUID: See **amorphous solid.**

SURFACE TENSION: The **resultant force** at the surface of a liquid, due to the **cohesive forces** between the particles of the liquid.

AN INCLINED PLANE

TEMPERATURE: How hot or cold a substance is. Temperature relates directly to the **kinetic energy** of a substance's particles. The particles in hotter objects have more kinetic energy.

TENSION: A **reaction force** in a solid that is stretched, which pulls the **atoms** of the solid together. It is the opposite of **compression**.

TERMINAL VELOCITY: The maximum speed attained by an object falling through a liquid or gas. A parachute falling through air has a relatively low terminal velocity, while that of a ball bearing will be much greater.

THERMAL EXPANSION: The expansion of a solid as its **temperature** increases. It is due to the increased vibration of the **atoms** and **molecules** of the solid. this increased vibration occurs at higher temperatures due to the increased **kinetic energy** of the atoms an molecules.

TOTAL INTERNAL REFLECTION: The reflection of light from the border between two materials, as the light passes from the denser to the less dense material.

MEASURING RESISTANCE

TURBINE: A machine in which a liquid or a gas causes rotation. When attached to a **generator**, the turbine helps to generate electricity.

UNIT CELL: The group of **atoms** or **molecules** in a crystal; when repeated, it forms the **crystal lattice**.

UPTHRUST: An upward **force** on an object immersed in a liquid or a gas. Upthrust is the **resultant** of the liquid or gas pressure acting on the object.

VELOCITY: The **speed** and direction of an object's motion.

VERNIER SCALE: A scale attached to instruments such as callipers, which allows very accurate measurements to be taken.

VOLTAGE: A measure of the **force** on particles with **electric charge**. The voltage in an **electric circuit** pushes **electrons** around the circuit.

VOLUME: The amount of space an object takes up.

WAVELENGTH: The distance from one wave peak to another. The wavelength of electromagnetic radiation determines the type of radiation. For example, X-rays have a shorter wavelength than light.

THE WEAK INTERACTION: A **force** between some types of particle, including **electrons**. Also involved in the decay of **hadrons**, such as the **beta decay** of **neutrons** in the **nucleus**. The force is carried by W and Z particles (see **gauge boson**).

WEIGHT: The **force** of **gravity** on an object, dependent on the mass of the object.

WORK: The amount of energy involved in a particular task. For example, work is said to be done when a pulley lifts a load. The amount of work done is equal to the force acting multiplied by the distance moved.

Index

Acknowledgments

Dorling Kindersley would like to thank:
Griffin and George, Loughborough, for the loan of scientific equipment;
University College London, for the loan of glassware; Maplin electronics,
Hammersmith

Special thanks to Lew Instone at Griffin and George, Peter Leighton at UCL,
and Patrick Rolleston at Kensington Park School

Additional design assistance:
Carla De Abreu, Anthea Forle

Additional editorial assistance:
Louise Candlish, Phillippa Colvin, Caroline Hunt, Jane Mason, Jane Sarluis,
Roger Tritton

Additional photography:
Tim Ridley

Model making:
Simon Murrell

Picture research:
Anna Lord

Picture credits:
CERN 50bl, 52br; Simon Fraser 37tr; Robert Harding/C. Delli 37cr; Image Bank/
Mel Digiacomo 47crb; Bruce Iverson 44c; Newage International Ltd 36tc;
Omikron 52cr; David Parker 39tc; Des Reid/Marian Tully 24tr; John Sanford 45tr;
Science Photo Library/Lawrence Berkeley Laboratory 52tr; Stammers/Thompson
39bc; Zefa 29bc, 35cl, 37c
(t=top, b=bottom, c=center, l=left, r=right)